QUICK & EASY PROJECTS
FOR THE WEEKEND
CARPENTER

QUICK & EASY PROJECTS
FOR THE WEEKEND CARPENTER

*Over 25 simple & stylish pieces
to make for your home*

ALAN & GILL BRIDGEWATER

BARRON'S

All inquiries should be addressed to:
Barron's Educational Series, Inc.
250 Wireless Boulevard
Hauppauge, New York 11788
http://www.barronseduc.com

Library of Congress Catalog Card No. 01-086494

International Standard Book No. 0-7641-1957-5

Printed in Singapore

10 9 8 7 6 5 4 3 2 1

AG&G Books would like to thank *Axminster™ Power Tool
Centre* for supplying the pictures on pages 8 and 9.

The information in this book is true and complete to
the best of our knowledge. All recommendations are
made without guarantee on the part of the authors
and the publishers. The authors and publishers disclaim
any liability for damages or injury resulting from the
use of this information.

Contents

Introduction

Sometimes, when I am busy in my workshop, with the warm, nutty smell of wood filling the air, I think about all the pleasures of woodwork. Of course the hands-on procedures are fun to do, but on top of that, I am always amazed by the fact that I may have a whole heap of wood stacked in the corner on one day, and by the next it has been transformed into a beautiful piece of furniture. When I watch the various projects being used in the house, or when I give them to friends and family as gifts, it is very rewarding to know that, but for me, the items wouldn't exist.

The intention of this book is to share with you all the pleasures of building projects from wood. When I first sat down to think up the projects, I was overwhelmed with ideas—there were so many exciting possibilities. Aimed specifically at eager weekend carpenters, the projects are carefully directed, with plenty of options, thorough step-by-step directions, and most important of all, they can be made and finished in the space of a weekend. We have designed the projects so that they can be made by woodworkers at all levels, from inexperienced beginners with a basic tool kit, to more accomplished woodworkers who want to make something a little bit special. We show you, in hands-on-tool detail, how to make over 25 different projects, including a bright, painted stool for a child, a chair for the porch or conservatory, a table, a chest, a rustic French cupboard for the kitchen, and bread and cheese boards. Each project opens with an introduction to put the piece in context, and then we go straight into the making stages. There is a full-page photograph to show the piece in detail, step-by-step text and photographs, extensive tool, material and cutting lists, working drawings, design variations, and tip boxes. We have done our best to see that you have a wonderful woodworking time every weekend, from ordering wood to laying out the designs and working with the router.

So now it is time to roll up your sleeves and get down to the fantastic, finger-tingling adventure of weekend carpentry. Best of luck.

Alan& Gill

Tools and equipment

Woodworking is an incredibly rewarding activity, but only if you are using the right tools and equipment for the task. It's no good battling with the wrong-size bandsaw, or trying to smooth wood with a plane that is dull edged, and then deciding that woodworking is not for you. If you choose your tools with care, you will enjoy the experience of woodworking. Buy a basic tool kit to begin with and purchase additional tools when the need arises.

BASIC MACHINES

Traditionally, home woodworkers used hand tools—planes, saws, hand drills and so on—but there is now a shift to using small, basic machines to do some of the more tedious tasks. The following five machines are very useful: table saw, thickness planer, bandsaw, benchtop drill press, and scroll saw.

Table saw A table saw is a machine for sawing stock to width and length. It is a table with a saw blade at the center, a rip fence to the right-hand side, and a sliding table to the left. To use it, you true up one edge of the wood, set the rip fence to the desired width, and then use your hands and a push-stick to move the wood through. It's a good machine if you want to reduce costs by converting rough-sawn boards to various plank and batten widths.

Thickness planer A thickness planer is a combination machine that is designed to plane all sides and edges of the wood square to each other, working through each in turn. Professional woodworkers generally use two machines—a jointer and a planer—but home woodworkers usually opt for a dual-purpose thickness planer. There are many machines on the market, so spend time looking at the options.

1 **Table saw:** *A table saw is a useful machine, especially if you are going to do a lot of woodwork. It is mainly used for converting large boards into smaller sections, with the benefit of speed and accuracy.*

2 **Thickness planer:** *A thickness planer is used for reducing sections to the desired thickness (or width).*
3 **Jointer:** *A jointer establishes flat planed surfaces on a face and an adjacent edge.*

Bandsaw An electric bandsaw is a benchtop machine made up of a flexible, looped blade running over and being driven by two or more wheels. It is designed for cutting broad curves in thick-section wood. (Narrow blades suit tight curves in thin wood, while wide blades are better for broad curves in thick wood.) I use a small bandsaw fitted with a ¼ in. (10 mm) blade.

Benchtop drill press The benchtop drill press—sometimes also called a pillar drill—is a machine dedicated to drilling holes. While you might think that a small, hand-held electric drill is sufficient for this purpose, a good-size benchtop drill press is better, because it enables you to bore accurately placed holes every time. To use it, you fit the bit in the chuck, clamp the workpiece to the drill table, set the depth gauge, and then pull the capstan wheel to bore the hole. A benchtop drill press teamed with a forstner bit is a combination that is difficult to beat.

Scroll saw The scroll saw is a fine-bladed electric saw designed for cutting intricate curves in wood. Before using it, the blade is tensioned, and then the workpiece is fed towards the blade. In order to saw out a shape in the middle of a piece of wood, one end of the blade is detached and passed through a drilled hole.

SPECIAL MACHINES

There are of course many other types of woodworking machines—everything from joint cutters, sanders, and veneering presses through to spindle molders, tenon cutters, large and small lathes, and plenty more as well. Novice woodworkers usually find that they soon develop an interest and expertise in a particular area, so they then go on to buy appropriate small machines. For example, I very quickly became interested in wood-turning—so much so that I purchased a lathe, and then a large, slow-wheel grinder to sharpen my turning tools. If you get hooked on joint-making, for example, you might choose to buy a dedicated mortiser and a machine for cutting dovetails, and then a special machine to hone your chisels, and so on. My advice is that you should not rush out right away and start buying large pieces of machinery, because they might never get used. Also, don't be tempted to purchase small add-on attachments for your basic power tools (see page 10), because they can never perform as well as a dedicated machine. It is much better to borrow machines from your friends if they are necessary to follow these projects, and then to buy your own equipment when you fully appreciate your needs.

1 **Bandsaw:** *A bandsaw is ideal for reducing rough-sawn planks and cutting broad curves in thick wood.*
2 **Benchtop drill press:** *A benchtop drill press, used in conjunction with a forstner bit, enables you to make accurate, clean-sided holes.*
3 **Scroll saw:** *A scroll saw is the best machine for cutting tight curves and intricate fretwork designs.*

BASIC POWER TOOLS

Many novice woodworkers own an electric drill and various attachments such as a sanding disk, mini lathe, dovetail cutter, and drill stand, all of which work in conjunction with the drill. The problem with these add-ons is that although they do work, to a greater or lesser extent, the results are usually so disappointing that the woodworker soon becomes frustrated. My advice is to buy dedicated power tools, designed specifically to do a task, when you are confident that you can make good use of them. In the context of this book, the following six power tools are the ones to consider: cordless drill, jigsaw and sander (basic tools), router, miter saw, and biscuit joiner (special tools).

Cordless drill A cordless drill is a great tool that is perfect for jobs where you don't want to be hampered by a trailing power cable. I have two such drills—one small and the other large. My large drill has a torque control that allows me to use it both for drilling holes and for driving in screws. All I do is turn the numbered setting to suit the load and the depth of the screw, and then get on with the job. The battery size allows me to work for most of the day without recharging it. However Gill finds the weight of this drill a bit heavy on the wrists, and prefers to use the much smaller drill, which has the battery unit built into the handle. At the end of the day, you have to remember to plug the rechargeable battery into an outlet.

However, bear in mind that while a cordless drill does free the working area from power cables, the gearing of the drill requires that you work the holes in gentle stages, rather than single thrusts.

Jigsaw A jigsaw looks a little bit like a sander with a flat table on the underside, from which a blade protrudes. To use it, the saw table is set on the workpiece, with the blade not quite touching the wood to be cut, then the power is switched on and the tool is advanced. As the blade moves up and down, it swings from front to back so that it is clear of the wood on the down stroke. On most saws the table can be adjusted so that it tilts and allows you to cut at an angle of up to 45°. Some jigsaws

are able to cut a thickness of up to 4 in. (100 mm), so it is a very useful tool for most of the projects in this book.

Sander Modern sanders are really very sophisticated. You have a choice between wheel sanders, belt sanders, sanders with file-like fingers, random orbital sanders that fit in the palm of your hand, large high-powered sanders that are used for finishing wide areas, and so on. We have two machines: a large, flat sander that we use for working broad surfaces, and a little triangular palm-size sander that is good for rounding over edges and for getting into tight corners.

SPECIAL POWER TOOLS

Router A router is designed to do all the tasks that were once achieved by using a whole range of planes. Not so long ago, grooves, molding, rabbets, and tongues were cut with chisels and different-sized planes (with various universal and multi-planes coping with a number of tasks). Today, a router does all these things. There are two schools of thought about routers. One says that they are noisy, dusty, potentially very dangerous, altogether unpleasant, and the cutters are very expensive; the other says that they are wonderful. Using a router may not be as much fun as using a plane, and the results may not be any better, but there is no denying that they are much faster.

To perform the tasks, a router is fitted with cutters in various shapes and sizes, which are the reverse of the shape that you want to cut. So, for example, a tongue-shaped cutter will make a groove-shaped cut. A router can be used as a hand-held tool and run forward to make the cut, or it can be turned over and fitted in a router table, in which case the workpiece is moved so that it comes into contact with the cutter.

Miter saw Strictly speaking, a power tool is defined as a smallish, hand-held tool such as a router, drill, or sander, but some of the benchtop machines are now so small and portable that the distinction between them is becoming blurred. The miter saw looks a bit like a cross between an angle grinder and a guillotine. It is primarily designed to crosscut, but you can also cut miters and angles up to 45°. The piece of wood is set on the table, the power is switched on, and the blade is lowered or pulled across the wood.

Biscuit joiner The biscuit joiner, or biscuiter, is a versatile, easy-to-use tool. You simply make marks on the two pieces of wood that you want to join (edge to edge or at right angles), then set the joiner on the mark, press the button, and push forward. This causes a saw wheel to make a groove. Next, you align grooves in both pieces of wood, fill them with glue, slide in a little biscuit-shaped piece of compressed wood, and clamp the wood together. This forms a reinforced joint.

Useful power tools: *1 Jigsaw for cutting curves, 2 Router for cutting grooves, joints, and edge profiles (cutters: 3 Radius cutter for routing an edge profile, 4 Straight cutter for trimming edges, 5 Straight cutter for routing grooves and housings, 6 Chamfer cutter for routing a 45° bevel), 7 Palm sander for smoothing flat or shaped surfaces (with 8 Sanding sheet), 9 Rechargeable drill and screwdriver.*

WORKING SAFELY

Woodworking is potentially dangerous so always follow this safety checklist:
- Do not use machinery if you are too tired to concentrate or taking medication that makes you drowsy.
- Study the machine manuals.
- Keep electric cables and plugs on power tools in good condition.
- Let someone in the house know when you are using any machines.
- Make sure you are adequately protected with a dust mask, goggles, and hearing protection (see page 13).
- If you have long hair, tie it back.
- Supervise children.
- Keep a first-aid kit nearby.
  - Be near a telephone in case of accidents.
  - Keep the workshop locked.

HAND TOOLS

Weekend carpenters need a good range of hand tools, including measuring tools, saws, planes, chisels, hammers, mallets, knives, and clamps.

Measuring tools Woodwork starts with measurements and guidelines. You will need a tape measure, pencils and ruler, a square, set square and bevel gauge for establishing angles, dividers for marking measurements, a compass for drawing circles, and a mortise gauge for laying out joints.

Saws The most useful saws to purchase are a tenon saw for sawing small sections of wood to length and for cutting large details, a gents saw for small joints, and a miter frame saw for cutting angles. Always choose best-quality saws that can be re-sharpened.

Planes You need three planes: a good smoothing plane for leveling board widths, planing edges, and for skimming the ripples that can occur on machine-planed wood, a block plane for cleaning up end grain and for planing through tenons flush with a surface, and a spokeshave for planing curves.

Chisels A set of good-quality chisels is essential. While there are all types of chisels on the market, I recommend that you get yourself a set of bevel-edge chisels—the best that you can afford. It is also useful to have a sharpening stone.

Frequently used hand tools and drill bits:
1 mallet, 2 miter frame saw, 3 quick-release clamp, 4 sash clamp, 5 metal rule or straightedge, 6 smoothing plane, 7 hammer, 8 bevel gauge, 9 mortise gauge, 10 square, 11 file, 12 turning tool, 13 spokeshave, 14 block plane, 15 tape measure, 16 dividers,

17 compass, 18 pencil, 19 large penknife, 20 small penknife, 21 forstner drill bit, 22 Phillips screwdriver, 23 twist bit, 24 plug cutter, 25 countersink bit, 26 allen key wrench, 27 long-nosed pliers, 28 adjustable wrench, 29 electric soldering iron, 30 bevel-edge chisel, 31 gents saw, 32 tenon saw, 33 small hacksaw.

Hammers and mallets I use three different hammers: a large claw hammer for heavy work and for pulling out nails, and a couple of different-sized hammers for all the small nailing tasks. A mallet is suitable for the times when you need to strike the wood or a tool and be certain that it will not cause damage or leave a mark. A carpenter's square-headed mallet is ideal for tapping chisels; a heavy, round-headed mallet provides more weight, or is good when using carving gouges.

Knives Knives are extremely useful tools. A good selection might include a small penknife for whittling, an old chip-carving knife for marking and for cleaning tasks, and a large, bevel-bladed knife for cutting dowels. I find that an old knife tends to keep its edge longer. These can often be found in junk shops.

Clamps You can never have too many clamps. I use several long-beam sash clamps, a holdfast clamp on the workbench alongside the vice, one or two new quick-release clamps, and a whole host of C-clamps that I have collected over the years. Only buy the best, always get them in pairs, and don't be tempted to purchase them secondhand, or to buy cheap imports.

Metalworking tools As well as the woodworking tools, you will also need a small hacksaw for trimming nails and cutting threaded metal rod to length, a file for smoothing the sawed edges of these, and pliers for any number of tasks. (I also use an electric soldering iron for pyrography: it is not really designed for the task, but it is safe and it does the job efficiently.)

OTHER TOOLS

Drill bits You need twist bits for drilling general holes, and large-size forstner bits to make special holes that form part of the design. If you can afford it, get yourself a whole range of forstner bits. They are expensive, but last well and cut a perfect hole every time. You will also need a countersink bit for drilling screwholes for countersunk screws, and a counter-bore bit and matching plug cutter for making a screw joint that incorporates a recess for a wooden plug.

Woodturning tools If you want to try your hand at woodturning, you will first need a lathe, plus a selection of woodturning tools including gouges for rouging out, a skew chisel for cutting grooves and for smoothing up, a parting tool for parting off, and a couple of scrapers for general smoothing and cleaning up. Start by making do with the tools supplied with the lathe, and then get yourself a better range when you have more experience and can decide what you really need.

SAFETY EQUIPMENT

When working with machines that make a lot of noise and produce fine dust, you need, at the very least, to get yourself a basic dust mask, a pair of hearing protectors, and a pair of safety goggles. I have also invested in a full-face respirator for working with the lathe. This mask not only allows me to wear my glasses, but it filters the air without the need to have something pressing directly against my mouth. There is one further health consideration: sometimes exotic species of wood cause allergic reactions. I avoid this possibility by mostly limiting myself to using pine (American or European pine).

Safety equipment: *1 full-face respirator with built-in visor, dust filter and air blower, 2 hearing protectors, 3 dust mask for low levels of wood dust, 4 goggles.*

Materials

It is best to purchase wood from a specialist supplier—a company that only sells wood and related products and tools. Do not expect the local home improvement center to supply everything you require or to have a detailed knowledge of the products on sale. For the projects in this book, I advise you to purchase your wood ready prepared, and as near as possible to the finished size. Inspect the wood for sale closely and reject pieces that are split, of poor color, twisted, full of knots, or in any way defective. If a piece of wood looks uncharacteristic, keep on searching. Go armed with a cutting list and a tape measure, and be clear in your own mind as to your needs. The ideal supplier is the sort of establishment staffed by friendly, knowledgeable people, who are prepared to cut the wood to size without splintering the cut edges, and can ensure that all the edges are square to each other. Certainly you will pay extra, but you won't be paying for wood that can't be used. Always ask for the scraps.

WOOD TYPES

Western pine A straight-grained, cream-colored softwood. It is easy to work, with an attractive grain texture and a minimum of knots—a perfect choice for most of the projects in this book.

Laminated pine Whenever I have trouble getting a board wide enough, I generally use laminated pine. The pine is sawed into strips and glued to a prepared board width. It's a good product for component parts such as the sides of chests. Avoid using laminated pine for outdoor furniture.

Ash A long-grained, tough, gray to red-brown hardwood traditionally used when there is a need for strength. A good choice for many of the projects.

Maple A cream-colored hardwood—perfect for modern furniture. I used it for the kitchen cart. It cuts to a beautiful crisp finish.

American oak Sometimes known as American red oak, this hardwood is pink-brown in color, with a beautiful straight grain. Although it is a very tough wood, it's also relatively easy to work.

American cherry A creamy pink-to-brown, fine-textured, straight-grained hardwood. It is expensive, but a good choice if you require a hard, shiny finish. Specify American cherry, because it comes in much wider boards than the European species.

American mahogany A red-brown, straight-grained, uniform-textured hardwood. I avoid using mahogany, because it is an endangered species and I don't like all the fine dust, but I sometimes use scraps salvaged from old doors. It's a good choice for very small details.

READY-PREPARED WOOD

Ready-prepared wood is planed and squared on all faces to a set width. You can also order it sized, and it will be sawed to a set length. However, if you enjoy the prospect of sawing and planing, just order the wood seasoned and sawed. When it comes to using tongue-and-groove boards (as in the French Cupboard), I go for best-quality prepared double-sided pine boards.

PLYWOOD

The projects in this book use top-quality birch plywood, which is a sheet material made up from veneer layers. It is easy to work—it saws and planes to a clean edge, and the light-colored grain is very attractive.

SAMPLES OF WOOD TYPES AND FINISHES

Wood types (and finishes): *1 Western pine (teak oiled), 2 Ash (teak oiled), 3 Maple (teak oiled), 4 American oak (Danish oiled), 5 American cherry (Danish oiled), 6 American mahogany (Danish oiled), 7 American oak (wire-brushed and oiled), 8 Western pine (colorwashed), 9 Western pine (acrylic paint).*

FASTENERS

There are literally thousands of products on the market, but I generally limit myself to using steel and brass screws, nails, and brads, plated steel threaded rod that I cut to length and use with washers and nuts, hex-head and toggle fasteners, wooden dowels, and plastic screw blocks. The brass hex-heads used in conjunction with the toggles and threaded rod may be unfamiliar to you. If you look at the Adjustable Porch Chair on pages 130–135, you will see how these beautiful fasteners allow boards to be joined at right angles to each other, without the need to cut traditional joints, and with the added benefit that the structure can be disassembled for easy transport. Note that most modern fasteners for making joints are designed to be hidden from view.

HARDWARE

The projects use four primary fittings: two different-shaped hinges (surface-mounted and recessed), brass cuphooks, and swivel wheels. There is not much to say about these items, other than they are best purchased when the project has been made, so that you can order a specific size and shape to fit the finished sizes. When you are buying hinges, obtain screws to fit at the same time. When it comes to knobs and handles, I much prefer to whittle my own from scraps of wood—as used on the Bathroom Cabinet (pages 88–93) and the French Cupboard (pages 124–129). I select a promising piece of wood, either a piece of straight-grained pine or a piece of basswood, and then simply whittle away with a penknife until I have a shape that I like.

Useful fasteners and hardware: *1 Plastic joining blocks, 2 Brass cuphook, 3 Swivel wheel, 4 Wooden fluted dowel, 5 Brass hex-head nut, 6 Toggle fastener, 7 Nut, 8 Washer, 9 Threaded rod (available in 36 inch (1 m) lengths), 10 Finishing nail, 11 Galvanized flat-headed nail, 12 Black steel brad, 13 Brass round-headed pin, 14 Slotted round-headed screw, 15 Slot-headed countersunk screw, 16 Phillips flat-head screw, 17 Phillips round-head screw, 18 Surface-mounted hinge, 19 Recessed hinge with countersunk screwholes.*

GLUE

There are hundreds of types of glue on the market, but there is no technical reason why, for the projects in this book, you shouldn't use white PVA glue. Squeeze it straight from the plastic bottle and spread it over both mating surfaces, and then clamp them and leave to cure.

FINISHING

Fortunately, thick, brown, high-shine varnishes are no longer in fashion. Instead we can use traditional finishes such as teak oil and Danish oil, or colorwashes in conjunction with oil and beeswax. The trouble with varnish is that you have to be careful there aren't any dribbles, and make sure that dust doesn't settle during the drying process. With oil, you don't have to worry about these things. I use teak oil and Danish oil straight from the bottle, either wiped on with a cloth or applied with a brush. Catalyst (two-part) lacquers are excellent spray finishes but unsuitable for the home workshop as special ventilation is required. Colorwash is made from acrylic paint thinned down with water. If I want to achieve a sheen finish, I simply wait for the oil or paint to dry, rub down with graded sandpaper, and then burnish with pure beeswax polish.

Glue and finishing materials: *1 PVA glue, 2 Teak oil, 3 Acrylic colorwash, 4 Danish oil, 5 Buffing polishing cloth, 6 Lint-free cotton cloth, 7 Pure beeswax polish, 8 Sanding block, 9 Garnet paper, 10 Silicon-carbide paper, 11 Aluminum-oxide paper, 12 Wire brush.*

Basic techniques

Woodwork is a bit like a journey. It is wonderful to set out, and just as exciting to reach your destination, but a good part of the enjoyment is in all the adventures between start and finish. It is a great feeling when you present family or friends with something that you have made with your own two hands, but many of the procedures and techniques along the way are just as pleasurable. When I test the edge of a razor-sharp blade, smell the wood and feel its texture, and then go on to make a crisp, clean cut, it is very satisfying. The following section will show you how to use your tools to achieve the various forms, joints, and textures. If you are ever unsure about any procedures involving tools, or uncertain whether a type of wood is suitable, it is always a good idea to make a trial run on scraps of wood. Try and keep the workshop shipshape—some woodworkers start a fresh project by cleaning and sharpening hand tools, organizing the workshop, and cleaning woodworking machines.

PREPARING PIECES OF WOOD

When you have decided what you want to make, take your carefully selected pieces of planed wood and sort them into groups. Mark each piece so that you know how it fits into the scheme of things, noting the top, bottom, best faces, and edges. Use a pencil and ruler to measure the lengths. Take a set square and run the marked points around the wood, so that you know which parts need to be cut away. Use a compass to set out curves and dividers to transfer measurements from drawings to the wood.

If you need to reduce the width of a board or lay out a joint, adjust the marking gauge to the appropriate measurement and run the gauge along the wood to make a mark. Use the bevel gauge to lay out lines that are going to run at an angle to an edge.

If you have pairs of components, measure them at the same time so that they are identical (and remember to make them a mirror image of each other). When you are setting out a detailed joint, it helps if you score the lines with a knife. When you have laid out all the lines that make up the design, it is often a good idea to shade in the waste side of the cutting line, so that you know precisely where to run the saw cut.

CUTTING CURVED SHAPES

To cut a curve, you have a choice of using a jigsaw, a scroll saw, a bandsaw, or one of the hand saws. A jigsaw is best for cutting rough curves in thick wood, when the line of cut is well away from the edge of the workpiece (see Fig 1). Set the table part of the saw on the mark, switch on the power, and advance to make the cut. Jigsaws have a tilting base, which changes the angle of the saw cut, and many kinds of blades are available to suit the type and thickness of a material.

FIG 1

Use a scroll saw for cutting fine curves in wood less than 2 in. (50 mm) thick (see Fig 2). Fit a new blade and adjust the tension until the blade "pings" when plucked. Set the workpiece on the saw table, switch on the power, and run the workpiece into the blade. If you feel the wood running off course, or you see the blade bending, ease back and readjust the direction of approach. If you need to cut out a window shape, then you can do one of two things. Either run the cut in from an edge or, to avoid cutting the wood surrounding the window, drill a hole through the waste, and then unhitch the saw blade, pass it through the hole and re-tension as already described.

FIG 2

DRILLING HOLES

Use the benchtop drill press in conjunction with a forstner bit for drilling large holes that need to be pre-cisely placed and worked (see Fig 3). Establish the center of the hole, fit the appropriate size bit, set the depth stop, and clamp the workpiece securely to the drill table. Clamping the workpiece takes a little extra time, but is worth doing because you can locate the hole more accurately, the finish of the hole will be better, and the procedure is safer. Lower the bit to ensure that the point is directly on center, then switch on the power and drill the hole through. If the hole is deep, lift the bit

out several times to remove the waste and to minimize overheating. If you are faced with drilling lots of holes in lots of identical component parts (see the Sauna Bench project on pages 98–101), it's a good idea to build a jig from scraps (a "fence" and a "stop" screwed to a base board, which is clamped to the drill table).

An electric drill used with a twist bit is a good option when you want to drill screwholes and perhaps pilot holes for nails. If you have a choice, use a cordless drill, so that you don't have to worry about the cable snaking around the workshop. To drill, you simply switch on the power, set the point of the bit on the mark, check to ensure that the bit is square to the face of the item being drilled, and then drill the hole through. When you have to put in a lot of screws (see Fig 4), a screwdriver drill attachment is very useful.

FIG 3

FIG 4

HAND PLANING

Hand planing is a very satisfying procedure, as long as the plane is sharp and you take your time. I use a smoothing plane for working in the direction of the grain (see Fig 5) along edges and faces. Make sure that the workpiece is secure, turn the brass advancing wheel to set the blade, perform a trial cut to judge whether or not the blade is at the correct depth, and then make the cut. When you are working the edge grain, hold the plane at a slightly skewed angle, with the fingers of your left hand under the sole of the plane to ensure that the plane is square to the face of the wood.

FIG 5

The block plane is perfect for trimming arris (sharp edge) details (see Fig 6) and for cleaning up end grain. Adjust the blade so that it makes the lightest of skimming cuts, try it on a piece of scrap, and then make the stroke. When you are working end grain, be careful not to run off course and split the grain (see Fig 7).

FIG 6

FIG 7

HAND CUTTING A MORTISE

Having used a pencil, ruler, set square and perhaps the point of a knife to lay out the mortise, move to the benchtop drill press and use the appropriate size bit to bore out most of the waste (see Fig 8). Be careful not to drill too near the edge of the mortise. Shake the waste from the hole, secure the workpiece in the vice so that the side to be worked is face up, and then take a suitable bevel-edge chisel and pare back the hole to the edge of the mortise (see Fig 9). Hold the chisel upright so that you don't undercut the surface or damage the edges. When you are half-way through, turn the wood over and work from the other side.

FIG 8

FIG 9

ROUTING A MORTISE

Depending on the size and position of the mortise, you can use a router to make the cut. You can either use the router as a hand-held tool and plunge down to clear the waste, or for an open-ended mortise (see Fig 10), you can attach the router to its table and run a groove from one end of the workpiece. In this instance, the accuracy of the cuts relates to the setting of the fence and the height of the bit. Always test your settings by routing a scrap piece (not a final component). It is best to cut the depth in stages, making several passes that do not overstrain the router. Make sure that you clear the waste after each pass to avoid overheating the bit.

HAND CUTTING A TENON

Begin by marking the shoulder-line (the length of the tenon) with a square and knife, and then mark the depth and width of the tenon with a marking gauge. Remove the waste with a tenon saw: first run a cut down the grain to the waste side of the gauged lines (stop the cut at the shoulder-line) on all four sides of the tenon. Cut across the grain to the waste side of the shoulder-line on all four sides, removing all the waste. Use a chisel to clean up the tenon and trim it to its proper size where necessary.

ROUTING A TENON

If you have a lot of tenons to make (or if you just like using machines), a router set in a table is the ideal tool for the job, as long as your pieces of wood are of a size that can be supported by the table (bigger pieces of wood are best clamped to the bench and routed by hand). All you do is set the fence to the length of the tenon, adjust the router bit to the appropriate height, then hold the workpiece hard against the push-fence and clear the waste with a series of passes (see Fig 11). When the end of the tenon reaches the fence, you turn the workpiece over and re-run the procedure on the other side. If you stop just before the router bit reaches the shoulder-line, you can use a chisel to clean up.

FIG 10

FIG 11

ROUTING A GROOVE WITH THE GRAIN

To cut a groove that is ¼ in. (6 mm) wide, ⁵⁄₃₂ in. (4 mm) deep and lies ⅜ in. (10 mm) in from the edge of a board, follow these steps. Attach the router to its table and fit a ¼ in. (6 mm) groove cutter. Set the fence to ⅜ in. (10 mm). Adjust the cutter so that it stands ⁵⁄₃₂ in. (2 mm) higher than the router table. Switch on the power and push the wood along the fence to cut a groove to a depth of ⁵⁄₃₂ in. (2 mm) (see Fig 12). Switch off the power, and then set the cutter ⁵⁄₃₂ in. (2 mm) higher and re-run the pass to cut the groove to ⁵⁄₃₂ in. (4 mm).

ROUTING A RABBET ON THE END OF A BOARD

To cut a rabbet ⅜ in. (10 mm) wide and ⁵⁄₃₂ in. (4 mm) deep, follow this procedure. Use a straight cutter that is smaller than the width of the rabbet—for example ⁷⁄₃₂ in. (5 mm). Put the router in the router table and fit the cutter. Set the fence ⁷⁄₃₂ in. (5 mm) back from the rear edge of the cutter, and adjust the cutter height to ⁵⁄₃₂ in. (2 mm). Switch on the power. Hold the workpiece against the push-fence and make a cut that laps into the end of the board by about ⁷⁄₃₂ in. (5 mm). Re-run the cut—keeping the end of the board against the fence—to cut the full ⅜ in. (10 mm) width of the rabbet. Switch off the power, adjust the cutter to stand ⁵⁄₃₂ in. (4 mm) high, and repeat to complete the cut (see Fig 13).

ROUTING A HOUSING GROOVE FREEHAND

Clamp the workpiece to the bench. Fit a router cutter the same size or smaller than the width of the groove, and set the depth stop. Clamp a guide strip of wood across the workpiece parallel to the groove, so that the cutter will run up the waste side of the drawn line. Set the router down with the base pressed to the guide, switch on the power, and wait until the cutter is up to speed, then cut. If the cutter is smaller than the groove, shift the guide strip closer and repeat until the groove is the correct size (see Fig 14).

FIG 12

FIG 13

FIG 14

ROUTING EDGE PROFILES

Cutting an edge profile is one of the easiest routing procedures. Attach the router to its table and fit your chosen cutter—radius (see Fig 16), cove (see Fig 15), Roman, or other type. Use one with a pilot or bearing roller-tip. Move the fence so that it is well out of the way. Switch on the power and wait until the router is up to full speed. Now press the workpiece down on the table and run it repeatedly against the cutter. Work with an easy, firm motion so that the cutter enters on the left and exits on the right. Continue until the workpiece rubs up against the pilot or roller-tip, at which point the cutter will cease to cut. If the profiled edge looks burnt, the router cutter might be blunt, or you may be moving too slowly across the wood.

FIG 15

FIG 16

ROUTING WITH A TEMPLATE

A template is used when you want to produce a number of identically shaped components with a smooth routed finish on all the edges. The components first need to be sawed roughly to the shape required, leaving no more than ¼ in. (4–5 mm) of waste wood to be removed by the router. Fit a guide brush to the base of the router. Cut a template from sheet plywood, allowing for the collar, and pin it directly to the face of the wood that you want to cut. Switch on the power and wait for the cutter to get up to full speed, then follow the edge of the template to make the cut.

A similar, but more immediate technique for duplicating a component uses the router, a straight cutter with a bearing attached (the bearing can be at the top or bottom of the cutter), and the original finished component, which is used as the template. The procedure is the same as that described above.

CUTTING MITERS WITH A FRAME SAW

The frame saw is an easy way of achieving angled saw cuts. Adjust the saw blade within the frame to your chosen angle—90°, 45°, 36°, 22.5°, or 15°—and lock it in place. Set the depth stop to the chosen depth. Position the workpiece on the saw table, firmly against the fence, and then gently run the saw backward and forward to make the cut (see Fig 17).

FIG 17

23

NAILING

Look at the workpiece to decide where the nail or brad is to be sited. If it is near an edge or end, where there is a chance that the wood will split, or you want to ensure that the nail goes in straight, run a pilot hole through with an electric drill, using a bit that is slightly smaller than the diameter of the nail. Set the point of the nail in the hole and use an appropriate size hammer to drive it in. Give it a series of well-placed taps (see Fig 18), all the while watching to make sure that the point of the nail doesn't break through the other side. If it does run off course, use a pair of pliers or a claw hammer to draw it out. If you are using very small brads, which are difficult to hold and hammer in, use a pair of long-nose pliers to grip the brad as you nail.

FIG 18

SCREWING

You have a choice of using mild steel, stainless-steel, brass, or aluminium screws (either Phillips head or slotted head) with various countersunk or domed heads. Dome-headed screws stand on the surface of the wood; countersunk screws are set flush with the surface, or held in a brass cup, or hidden by a plug of wood. Screws are driven in with a Phillips or flat screwdriver, either by hand or using an electric drill fitted with a screwdriver bit (see Fig 19). If you use a screwdriver bit in an electric drill, set the slipping clutch mechanism so that the screw is driven in to the correct

depth. If the wood is soft, you can make a pilot hole with an awl (see Fig 20); if it is hard you can bore a pilot hole with a small drill bit. If you want to cover the screws with a wood plug, you will need a counter-bore bit to drill the pilot hole and the hole for the plug, and a matching plug cutter to cut the plug. I find it is best to practice the entire drilling and screwing operation on a piece of the scrap. Do not use steel screws for oak, because they react with the wood and moisture to leave a stain. Use plated steel, brass, or stainless-steel screws instead.

FIG 19

FIG 20

WOODTURNING

If you want to make true round-section items such as chair legs, bowls, and platters, the only way to do it is to turn them on a lathe. Buy the highest powered, heaviest lathe that you can afford—one with an expanding chuck and a selection of face plates. Spindles and cylinders are pivoted and turned between the head center and the tailstock center (see Fig 21), while bowls and dishes are generally turned on a flat face plate. The best lathes are fitted with a device that allows you to turn large face-plate items on the outboard end of the drive spindle (see Fig 22). You will need various turning tools: a gouge, parting tool, skew chisel, and a round-nosed scraper. Lathes can be very dangerous, so always follow the safety instructions.

FIG 21

FIG 22

WHITTLING

All you need for whittling items such as door knobs and catches is a good, sharp knife (not stainless steel). The wood should be a smooth-grained variety. Take the wood in one hand and the knife in the other, and work with a series of tight, paring, thumb-pushing strokes (see Fig 23). The only way to become good at whittling is to get plenty of practice. In the first instance, try working with a piece of basswood.

FIG 23

ATTACHING HINGES

We use two hinge types: decorative brass hinges that are surface mounted with countersunk screws set flush with the hinge plate, and steel hinges set in a recess and attached with countersunk steel screws. To recess a hinge, mark around the flap with the point of a fine-bladed knife, use a chisel to chop down to the waste side of the scored line, and finally skim out the waste with a sharp chisel. Work cautiously so that the hinge is a tight push-fit in the recess, and take care to control the chisel so that it doesn't lift the surrounding grain. If you are worried about recessing a hinge, then either make several trial runs on scrap wood until you get it right, or opt for hinges that sit flush with the surface. There are a lot of different designs on the market, so you can easily choose a type that suits your needs and skill level. Always obtain screws at the same time as the hinges, to ensure that the countersink is compatible.

SANDING

The sanding or rubbing procedure involves using a variety of sandpapers to produce a smooth finish. Use the sandpaper as it is or fold it around a sanding block (see Fig 24), or use an electric sander (see Fig 25). I usually sand several times during a project—when the edges have been sawed, after the glue has cured, and before and after the final finish. I tend to use ordinary sandpaper for the initial rubbing, and fine-grade aluminium oxide paper when I want to achieve a special finish. Aluminium oxide paper is more expensive than sandpaper, but it lasts much longer. My favorite electric sander is an orbital type which is really good for large, flat surfaces. When you are sanding, work in a ventilated area and wear a dust mask (see page 13).

NATURAL FINISHES

A natural finish literally means that the wood is sanded and then left in its natural state, but the term has also come to mean a surface that has been oiled or waxed. Danish oil and teak oil can be applied with a lint-free cotton cloth or a brush (see Fig 26). You apply a thin coat, let it dry, wipe it with the finest grade of sandpaper to remove the "fuzz" (the rough texture created by raised wood fibers that are left after the first coat of oil has soaked in), and then apply another thin coat. If you want to soften the surface, you can follow the second rubbing down with wax polish.

For projects that come into direct contact with food, replace teak or Danish oil with a vegetable oil. I use ordinary olive oil wiped on with a cloth (see Fig 27).

FIG 24

FIG 26

FIG 25

FIG 27

PAINTED FINISH

When it comes to painting a solid color you have a choice between using oil-based paint (see Fig 28) or water-based acrylic paint. Both paints need to be carefully applied with a brush. Though there is very little visual difference between the end results produced by the two types of paint, brushes used for oil paint need to be cleaned with mineral spirits, while those used for acrylic paint can be cleaned under running water. Currently, I choose paints for their depth and quality of color, rather than for anything else. As for the side-effects of working with paint, I find that oil fumes tend to make me woozy, while acrylic fumes dry my throat. My advice is to wear a mask to protect you from toxic vapors whichever paint you are using, and as far as possible, to do the painting out in the open.

FIG 28

SPECIAL FINISHES

When using American oak, you can obtain an interesting finish by scouring the grain with a wire brush. I particularly like the feel of a wire-brushed finish, and the rugged surface means that I don't have to worry about my dogs' paws damaging it. The wire brush is rubbed in the direction of the grain (see Fig 29) until the soft areas break down, and the wood is finished with oil.

The candle-smoking technique is fun to do and perfect for covering up a poor-grade wood. Brush the painted surface with oil-based varnish, wait for it to become tacky, and then play the candle flame over the surface (see Fig 30). Always wait for the surface to go tacky (so that it just takes a fingerprint), and always keep the can of varnish and the brushes well away from the candle. This is a procedure that is best managed with a friend's help, in an area well away from the workshop. Practice on scrap wood before you start.

FIG 29

FIG 30

KEY TO THE PROJECTS

Ideal beginner's project

Perfect for those who have some experience of woodworking

Ambitious projects, which experienced carpenters will enjoy

Tableware

We all enjoy sitting around a table and sharing a meal with family and friends. But just think how much more fun it would be if you could boast that you had made the tableware. This project involves making two items: oak eggcups that double as napkin rings, and heart-shaped plywood table mats with their own rack. The designs are somewhat kitsch, but the fact that the shapes and the colors are exaggerated is part of their appeal, and children will love them too. Also, both eggcups and mats are very practical, and perfect for a young family.

The woodworking techniques are amazingly easy—just a case of drilling large holes and fretting the plywood on the scroll saw. The painting is slightly more difficult and needs to be done with care. When the project is finished, and the items are being used at the breakfast table, don't be surprised to see your children piling the eggcups into stacks and playing with the heart shapes—take it as a sign that they are a success!

─────────── Essential Tools ───────────

workbench with vise and holdfast, compass,
pencil, ruler, square, benchtop drill press or electric drill,
1¾ in. (45 mm) forstner bit, clamps, sanding block, 1 in.
and ⅜ in. (25 mm and 10 mm) paintbrushes, scissors, scroll
saw, router and router table, ³⁄₁₆ in. (5 mm) radius cutter,
³⁄₁₆ in. (5 mm) and ⁵⁄₁₆ in. (8 mm) twist bits, countersink bit,
medium-size hammer

OTHER USEFUL TOOLS
cordless screwdriver, power sander, dividers,
marking knife

Tableware

1¾ in.
(45 mm) hole

2 in. (50 mm)

2⅝ in.
(65 mm)

2⅝ in.
(65 mm)

**You'll need
to know**

DRILLING HOLES
p.19

ROUTING EDGE
PROFILES
p.23

CUTTING CURVED
SHAPES
p.18

*This eggcup/napkin ring design relies on
the block of wood being in perfect condition—
there must be absolutely no splits running
into the end grain.*

Materials

oak and plywood (see cutting list)
sandpaper grades 80 and 120
acrylic paint: four colors to suit
clear oil-based gloss varnish
thin paper and cardboard
2 x 2¾ in. (70 mm) lengths ⁵⁄₁₆ in. (8 mm) dowel
PVA glue
gloss paint: bright red
mineral spirits to clean the brushes

Cutting List

6 pieces oak 2⅝ × 2⅝ × 2 in. (65 × 65 × 50 mm)
(eggcup blocks)

1 piece plywood 10¼ × 9⅞ × ½ in.
(260 × 250 × 12 mm) (heart rack back board)

1 piece plywood 8⅝ × 8¼ × ½ in.
(220 × 210 × 12 mm) (heart rack front board)

6 pieces plywood 8⅝ × 8¼ × ¼ in.
(220 × 210 × 6 mm) (heart mats)

9⅞ in.
(250 mm)

10¼ in.
(260 mm)

10¼ in.
(260 mm)

8¼ in.
(210 mm)

⁵⁄₁₆ in. (8 mm)
dowel

8⅝ in.
(220 mm)

5⅛ in.
(130 mm)

4¹⁵⁄₁₆ in. (125 mm)

4⅛ in. (105 mm)

8⅝ in.
(220 mm)

*The heart rack accommodates six table mats, but you
could easily increase the dimensions to suit your needs.
Use the template on the right to construct the heart
shapes [one grid square = approx ⅜ in. (10 mm)].*

EGGCUPS/NAPKIN RINGS

FIG 1

1 Take your prepared oak blocks and check them over to make sure that they are free from cracks. Draw crossed diagonals to establish the position of the center points (see Fig 1). Do this on both sides of the block.

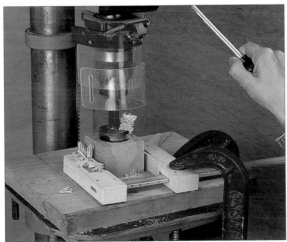

FIG 2

2 Fit the 1¾ in. (45 mm) forstner bit in the bench-top drill press. Secure the workpiece with clamps—one to grip the workpiece, another to hold the waste board down on the table, and another clamp to hold the gripping clamp. Drill a hole through the 2 in. (50 mm) thickness (see Fig 2). Keep clearing the waste so the bit does not overheat.

TIP

The only way of drilling a smooth-sided, large-diameter hole is to use a forstner bit. They are much more expensive than ordinary bits, but they will last a lot longer. When you bore out the holes, run the bit in little by little, so the waste is removed without overheating the bit.

FIG 3

3 Use the graded sandpapers to rub all the surfaces to a smooth finish. When you are happy with the results, wipe away the mess and move to a clean, dust-free area that you have set aside for painting. Take one block at a time and brush on the acrylic colors—make one side red, another side blue, and so on (see Fig 3). Continue until all the sides of all of the blocks are painted. When the paint is completely dry, use the finest grade of sandpaper to gently smooth the raised grain of the wood. Finally, give all the surfaces a coat of clear gloss varnish.

HEART TABLE MATS

FIG 1

FIG 3

4 Draw the two heart shapes on paper and then transfer to cardboard. Use the cardboard template to trace the shapes on the plywood (see Fig 1). Mark the shape with a single drawn line, so there is no doubting the line of cut.

6 Attach the router to its table and insert the radius cutter. Set the boards face down on the table and profile the edges so they are nicely rounded (see Fig 3). Do both sides of the heart front and back board that make the rack.

FIG 2

FIG 4

5 Cut out the eight hearts on the scroll saw— two from the ½ in. (12 mm) plywood, and six from the ¼ in. (6 mm). Run a cut straight in and out of the cleft at the top of the heart, and then work from the point back into the cleft (see Fig 2). Saw at a steady, easy pace, all the while making sure that the cut is to the waste side of the drawn line.

7 Draw in the position of the dowel centers on the hearts for the rack. Drill a pair of holes in the front board with the ⁵⁄₁₆ in. (8 mm) twist bit. Hold the two boards together with a length of dowel, and drill the other holes (see Fig 4). Drill out the two hanging holes with the ³⁄₁₆ in. (5 mm) twist bit and finish with the countersink bit.

FIG 5

FIG 6

8 Take the two 2¾ in. (70 mm) dowels and round over the ends with sandpaper. Set the back and front boards together on the dowels and fix them in place with glue. Use the hammer to nudge the boards about 1½ in. (38 mm) apart, so that the dowel ends protrude on the front face (see Fig 5), and wipe away the glue. Check to make sure that the rack holds all six mats comfortably.

9 Wipe away all traces of dust and move to a clean area that you have set aside for painting. Give all surfaces a couple of coats of bright red gloss paint (see Fig 6), so that the hearts look attractively shiny. Finally, when the paint is absolutely dry, rub the surfaces with the finest grade of sandpaper and give everything a coat of varnish. Sand and varnish again.

Construction variations

Two dowel pegs on a large heart-shaped board hung on the wall

The heart-shaped mats slot between the boards and rest on dowels

Each heart mat has two drilled holes so it can be hung from the dowels

Layered plywood construction forming a pocket for the mats

Two boards mounted to the wall with dowels

Kitchen wall rack

The wall rack is a great project for the kitchen. If you don't have anywhere to hang your pots and pans, and spoons, slicers, and spatulas are strewn across the worksurface, transform your life with this really attractive design feature that stores all the utensils at an easy-to-reach height. And if you enjoy drying herbs, or collecting and displaying antique utensils, the holes at the end of the slats and the brass cuphooks will come in extremely useful for hanging items, using a ribbon if necessary.

The wall rack is very easy to make—just a small amount of work on the scroll saw, and a bit of drilling. The success of the project relies on the spacing of the slats, which has to be just right, and the finish—you do need to take time with the sanding. The good thing about the design of the rack is its flexibility. For example, if you require a wider rack, all you do is add another vertical runner and lengthen the slats accordingly. Measure the wall space and adjust the overall size of the rack to fit. Check the position of water pipes and power cables before you screw the rack to the wall.

─────────── Essential Tools ───────────

workbench with vise and holdfast, compass, pencil, ruler,
square, clamp, scroll saw, benchtop drill press,
⅜ in., ³⁄₁₆ in., and ⅛ in. (10 mm, 5 mm, and 3 mm) twist
bits, electric drill, screwdriver, sanding block, paintbrush

OTHER USEFUL TOOLS
cordless screwdriver, power sander, marking knife, block
plane

Kitchen wall rack

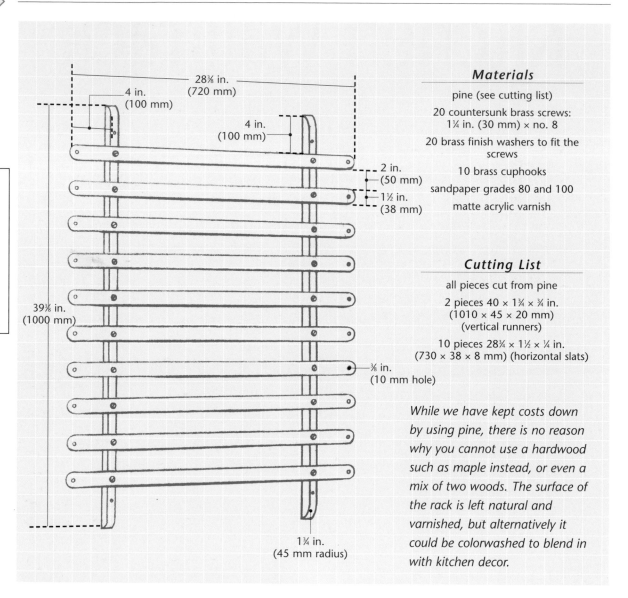

28⅜ in.
(720 mm)

4 in.
(100 mm)

4 in.
(100 mm)

2 in.
(50 mm)

1½ in.
(38 mm)

39⅜ in.
(1000 mm)

⅜ in.
(10 mm hole)

1¾ in.
(45 mm radius)

Materials

pine (see cutting list)

20 countersunk brass screws:
1¼ in. (30 mm) × no. 8

20 brass finish washers to fit the
screws

10 brass cuphooks

sandpaper grades 80 and 100

matte acrylic varnish

Cutting List

all pieces cut from pine

2 pieces 40 × 1¾ × ¾ in.
(1010 × 45 × 20 mm)
(vertical runners)

10 pieces 28¾ × 1½ × ¼ in.
(730 × 38 × 8 mm) (horizontal slats)

While we have kept costs down by using pine, there is no reason why you cannot use a hardwood such as maple instead, or even a mix of two woods. The surface of the rack is left natural and varnished, but alternatively it could be colorwashed to blend in with kitchen decor.

FIG 1

1 Check the prepared wood for possible problems such as splits and badly placed knots. While the runners can have a few knots here and there, it is most important that the slats are smooth grained along their length. If you have doubts about the quality of your wood, look for better stock. Take the two 40 in. (1010 mm) runners, set the compass to 1¾ in. (45 mm) and draw quarter-circle curves ³⁄₁₆ in. (5 mm) short of the ends. Use the scroll saw to cut the ends to shape (see Fig 1).

FIG 2

2 Take the slats and use the compass to set out circles 1⅜ in. (35 mm) in diameter on the ends. Have the circles set back 3⁄16 in. (5 mm) from the ends, so that the slats all finish up at 28⅜ in. (720 mm) long. On the benchtop drill press, run ⅜ in. (10 mm) holes through the center points (see Fig 2).

FIG 3

3 Cut the ends of the slats to shape on the scroll saw (see Fig 3). Do your best to cut slightly to the waste side of the drawn line, so that the curve is true. If you fit a new blade and work at an easy pace, the sawed edges will hardly need sanding. Make sure the blade is fitted so the teeth point down toward the table.

> ## TIP
>
> The trickiest part of this project is getting the whole thing true, so that the slats are horizontal to each other and square with the runners. The best way to do this is to lay out the dimensions on one runner (the width of the slats and the spacing) and then to clamp the two runners side by side and run the lines across with the square. This way of working ensures that both pieces of wood are set out with an identical pattern of guidelines.

FIG 4

4 Mark guidelines on the runners, spacing the slats 2 in. (50 mm) apart. For each screw, drill 3⁄16 in. (5 mm) holes through the slats and ⅛ in. (3 mm) pilot holes into the runners. Fix the slats with the screws and finish washers (see Fig 4). Sand all the surfaces, fit the cuphooks, and varnish the whole wall rack. The end grain might need a couple of coats.

Tea tray

The styles of the 1950s do not excite everyone, but there is something about the simplicity of the period that is very appealing. Designers of the time experimented with smooth curves, new materials such as plastics, and lots of primary colors, making many of the household items appear quite daring. This little 1950s-style tray is also quite different from the ornate mahogany and brass of earlier times, instead using a sheet of plywood with simple strip wood handles. We have chosen white and red enamel paint—which would have been just right for the red-and-white kitchens of the 1950s—but you may prefer to select an alternative color scheme.

The procedures are very easy. All the parts are cut out on the scroll saw, the individual components are painted, and then the tray is put together with brass screws. What could be easier? That said, the success of the project relies on the sawed lines being crisp and clean, and the paint finish being smooth and free from runs and drips. If you have doubts about your painting skills, practice on a piece of scrap wood first.

Essential Tools

workbench with vise, compass, pencil, ruler,
square, scroll saw, sanding block, paintbrush,
electric drill, ⅛ in. (3 mm) twist bit,
countersink bit, screwdriver

OTHER USEFUL TOOLS
cordless screwdriver, power sander, dividers,
marking knife, block plane

Tea tray

You'll need to know

CUTTING CURVED
SHAPES
p.18

PAINTED FINISHES
p.27

SCREWING
p.24

12 in.
(300 mm)

¾ in.
(20 mm)
radius

⅜ in.
(10 mm)
radius

18 in.
(460 mm)

½ in.
(15 mm)

¾ in.
(20 mm)

1 in.
(25 mm)

15 in.
(380 mm)

1 in.
(25 mm)

5½ in.
(140 mm)

8¾ in.
(220 mm)

1½ in.
(40 mm) radius

If you make the tray larger, increase the dimensions of the handle strips so that they are strong enough to carry a heavier weight.

Materials

plywood and pine (see cutting list)

sandpaper grade 100

gloss paint: red and white

mineral spirits to clean the brush

12 countersunk brass screws:
⅝ in. (15 mm) × no. 8

Cutting List

1 piece of plywood
18 × 12 × ¼ in.
(460 × 300 × 6 mm)
(baseboard)

2 pieces of pine
15 × ¾ × ½ in.
(380 × 20 × 15 mm)
(side strips)

2 pieces of pine
8¾ × ¾ × ½ in.
(220 × 20 × 15 mm)
(handle strips)

FIG 1

FIG 2

1 Measure 1½ in. (40 mm) along from each end of the base board, rule a line across and draw the large circles 1½ in. (40 mm radius) and the smaller circles 8 in. (20 mm) radius. Set out the handles with radii of ⅜ in. (10 mm) and ¾ in. (20 mm) (see Fig 1).

2 Check against the working drawing to ensure that all is correct, and then cut out the parts on the scroll saw (base, handles, and side strips). The line of cut must be slightly to the waste side of the drawn line (see Fig 2).

FIG 3

3 Sand the sawed faces to a slightly round-edged finish. Paint the parts with the gloss paint—red for the side and handle strips and white for both sides of the base. When the paint is completely dry, repeat the sanding with the finest grade of sandpaper (see Fig 3), and apply another thin coat of paint.

FIG 4

4 Mark the position of the side and handle strips on the baseboard and drill ⅛ in. (3 mm) pilot holes through the base and about 3/16 (5 mm) into the strips. Countersink the base holes on what will be the underside of the tray, and finally screw the strips in place (see Fig 4).

Construction variations

Handle shape drawn with compass and cut from thick plywood

Side pieces with rounded tops

Mitered joint at the corners

Handle area cut from base and side piece

Curved wood handle screwed to the side pieces

Base with rounded corners and rounded edges

Console shelf

This project was inspired by the painted folk art woodwork that was made in America in the nineteenth century by the German settlers in Pennsylvania. It was characterized by very simple construction, using lots of nails, and was painted either with brightly colored motifs and designs, or given an overall texture to fool the eye into believing that it was made from an exotic wood.

This particular little shelf is decorated by a technique known as candle marbling or smoking. The wood is painted with a base color, usually red, blue or green, and then, when the paint is dry, the surface is brushed with oil-based varnish, left until it is tacky, and finally the tip of the flame of a lighted candle is played over the surface. The black carbon from the flame bleeds into the varnish to create a shimmering, opalescent blue-black effect, a bit like the bloom on a fresh black plum.

The shelf's construction is very basic. The three components are cut out on the scroll saw and then simply attached with screws that run down from the top and in from the back. The only slightly more ornate piece of woodwork is the cyma curve bracket that supports the shelf.

Essential Tools

workbench with vise, compass, pencil, ruler, square,
scroll saw, router and router table, ¼ in. (6.3 mm)
radius cutter, sanding block, hand drill, ⅛ in. (3 mm)
twist bit, countersink bit, screwdriver, 2 paintbrushes

OTHER USEFUL TOOLS
cordless screwdriver, power sander, electric drill,
dividers, marking knife, block plane, tenon saw

Console shelf

11¹³⁄₁₆ in.
(300 mm)

6 in.
(150 mm)
radius

5⁵⁄₁₆ in.
(135 mm)
radius

10⅝ in.
(270 mm)

The console shelf is screwed together:
2 screws attach the back to the bracket,
3 screws attach the shelf to the back and
1 screw attaches the shelf to the bracket.
Below: template for the bracket.

4⅜ in.
(110 mm)

4⅜ in.
(110 mm)

Materials

pine (see cutting list)
sandpaper grades 80 to 150
6 countersunk steel screws: 1¼ in. (30 mm) × no. 8
matte, oil-based tile paint: red
oil-based clear varnish
mineral spirits to clean the brushes
large candle

Cutting List

all pieces cut from pine
1 piece 11¹³⁄₁₆ × 6�` × ¾ in. (300 × 160 × 18 mm)
(shelf board)
1 piece 10⅝ × 5½ × ¾ in. (270 × 140 × 18 mm)
(backboard)
1 piece 4⅜ × 4⅜ × ¾ in. (110 × 110 × 18 mm)
(bracket board)

FIG 1

1 Use the compass to set out the shelf board at a radius of 6 in. (150 mm), and the backboard at 5⁵⁄₁₆ in. (135 mm). Transfer the shape of the cyma curve to the bracket board (see Fig 1).

FIG 2

2 Cut out the three component parts on the scroll saw—the half-circle of the shelf board to a finished diameter of 6 in. (150 mm), the half-circle backboard to a diameter of 10⅝ in. (270 mm), and the right-angled cyma-curve bracket to measure 4⅜ in. × 4⅜ in. (110 mm × 110 mm) (see Fig 2).

FIG 3

3 Insert the radius cutter in the router and attach the router to its table. Cut radius curves on the underside of the shelf and on the front of the backboard (see Fig 3).

FIG 4

4 Use the sanding block and fine-grade sandpaper to sand everything to a smooth finish. Pay particular attention to the edge of the shelf and the sawed edges of the cyma curve (see Fig 4). Drill ⅛ in. (3 mm) pilot holes for the screws and countersink with the countersink bit.

FIG 5

5 Have a trial fitting to make sure that everything is correct, and then screw the pieces together. The screws run through the backboard into the bracket, and through the shelf board into the top edge of the backboard and into the bracket (see Fig 5).

FIG 6

6 Paint the shelf red. When the paint is dry, apply a thin coat of varnish. When the varnish is tacky and almost dry, light the candle and play the tip of the flame over the surface to create the marbled effect (see Fig 6). Be careful not to overdo the smoking, especially at the edges, or it will obliterate the red color. Finally, give the shelf a second coat of varnish.

TIP

Caution—keep the varnish and mineral spirits away from the lighted candle, because both are highly flammable. The varnished surface must be tacky before you start the candle work, or you won't achieve the correct result.

Colonial wall shelf

The houses of early settlers in America were filled with all types of shelves. There were console shelves for candles, shelves for bags and pouches, shelves for storing dry goods, and so on. All were put together with the minimum of joints, and charmingly decorated in a naïve style. The shelf in this project beautifully recreates the work of the New England craftsmen, who were masters of compass work and the cyma curve.

The low-tech housing groove and glued construction make the shelf a great project for beginners who have a relatively limited tool kit. Pine is used throughout, making it economical to build. The decoratively shaped edges turn it into a very attractive piece, so it would be perfect for a living room display shelf. The side boards are cleverly designed so that the symmetrical shapes are easy to achieve by eye and with a compass. All you do is draw the design on one side of the centerline and then trace it and flip it over to the other side. Make sure that the shaped edges of the side boards are free from knots and splits, especially the curves lying just in front of the shelves.

───────── Essential Tools ─────────

workbench with vise and holdfast, compass,
pencil, ruler, square, scroll saw, router and router table,
½ in. (13 mm) groove cutter, clamps, knife, sanding
block, paintbrush, screwdriver

OTHER USEFUL TOOLS
cordless screwdriver, power sander, marking knife,
block plane

Colonial wall shelf

6⅞ in.
(175 mm)

4⅜ in.
(110 mm)

4⅜ in.
(110 mm)

17½ in.
(440 mm)

4⅜ in.
(110 mm)

4⅜ in.
(110 mm)

6 in.
(158 mm)

12⅞⁄₁₆ in.
(316 mm)

¹¹⁄₁₆ in.
(17 mm)

6⅞ in.
(175 mm)

8¾ in.
(220 mm)

Materials

pine (see cutting list)
PVA glue
sandpaper grades 80 and 150
artist's oil paint: red, burnt umber and black
teak oil
mineral spirits to clean the brush

4 × 1¼ in. (30 mm) brass mirror hangers
with brass screws to fit

Cutting List

all pieces cut from pine

2 pieces 17½ × 6⅞ × ¾ in.
(440 × 175 × 18 mm) (side boards)

2 pieces 12 × 6 × ¾ in.
(300 × 158 × 18 mm (shelves)

We could have concealed the mirror hangers by placing them on the inside, but traditonally hangers were set as "ears," so they become a decorative detail, and we have followed suit.

You'll need to know

CUTTING CURVED SHAPES
p.18

ROUTING A HOUSING GROOVE
p.22

ROUTING A REBATE
p.22

FIG 1

FIG 2

1 Arrange the two 17½ in. (440 mm) sides so that the best edges are facing outward. Divide into four equal pieces and use the square, ruler and compass to lay out the design (see Fig 1).

2 Using the scroll saw, run a cut along the centerline, and then back out of the kerf (saw cut). Cut out the design, finishing in the cleft (see Fig 2). Do this for both side boards.

FIG 3

FIG 4

3 Use the router and ½ in. (13 mm) groove cutter to cut the housing grooves. Clamp a side board to the bench, and with waste strips in place, adjust the position of the guide to ensure that the router bit is perfectly on course. Set the depth guide to ⅜ in. (10 mm). Finally, switch on the power, hold the router base plate hard up against the guide strip, check that the flex is clear, and cut the housing groove (see Fig 3).

4 Mount the router on the router table. Set the fence to ⅜ in. (10 mm), and cut shoulders on the shelf ends (see Fig 4). Use the knife to whittle the shoulders to fit the stopped ends of the housing grooves. Glue and clamp together. Sand to a smooth finish. Mix a little of the red, black, and burnt umber paint into the teak oil, and brush on one or more coats. Screw the mirror hangers to the back edges of the side boards.

Construction variations

Housing joint runs right across the side and is visible at the front

Alternative shape for the sides

Profiled edge on the front of the shelves

Counterchanged design for the sides

Arts and Crafts mirror

The design of this mirror pays homage to Arts and Crafts designers such as Gustav Stickley and Ernest Gimson with its use of proportion, very slender through-tenons, the way the horizontal members extend beyond the limits of the frame, and the use of dowels to hold the joints together. However, although an Arts and Crafts form will happily blend into most homes, an altogether lighter feel—both in color and proportions—is perhaps more consistent with modern styles. So, instead of using thick-section oak, we have opted for using a much thinner section of straight-grained pine.

Made from pine throughout, with dowels standing proud and the back rabbeted to take the mirror glass, this is quite a challenging project. The tricky part is cutting the mortises through the thickness of the wood: you will be cutting a mortise ⁵⁄₁₆ in. (8 mm) wide through a ¾ in. (20 mm) piece of pine, with only a ⁷⁄₃₂ in. (6 mm) thickness of wood at either side of the mortise. It will test your skills! If you are not sure whether your woodworking expertise or your tools are up to it, make a trial run on scrap wood beforehand.

―――――― Essential Tools ――――――

workbench with vise and holdfast, compass, pencil, ruler, square, mortise gauge, clamps, benchtop drill press, ¼ in. and ½ in. (6 mm and 12 mm) forstner bits, mallet, ¼ in. (6 mm) and ¾ in. (20 mm) bevel-edge chisels, marking knife, router and router table, penknife, ⅜ in. (10 mm) groove cutter, block plane, small hammer, sanding block, screwdriver

OTHER USEFUL TOOLS
power sander

Arts and Crafts mirror

20 in.
(500 mm)

4 in.
(100 mm)

½ in.
(12 mm) dowel

28 in.
(700 mm)

20 in.
(500 mm)

¾ in.
(20 mm)

4 in.
(100 mm)

10½ in.
(260 mm)

4 in.
(100 mm)

4 in.
(100 mm)

Materials

pine (see cutting list)
PVA glue
sandpaper grades 80 and 150
beeswax polish and lint-free cotton cloth
mirror glass 20¾ × 11¼ × 3/16 in.
(520 × 280 × 5 mm)
6 mirror clips with screws to fit
2 brass screw eyes and brass picture wire: size and design to suit

Cutting List

all pieces cut from pine
2 pieces 28 × 4 × ¾ in.
(700 × 100 × 20 mm) (long sides)
2 pieces 20 × 4 × ¾ in.
(500 × 100 × 20 mm) (short sides)
8 × 1 in. (8 × 25 mm) lengths of
½ in. (12 mm) pine dowel

If you make the frame bigger, you will also need to increase the width and thickness of the wood.

FIG 1

FIG 2

1 Take the two 20 in. (500 mm) lengths of wood and use the square to position the mortises ¾ in. (20 mm) along from the ends. Set the spurs of the mortise gauge to 5/16 in. (8 mm) apart, and score the lines so that they are centered on the ¾ in. (20 mm) thickness of wood (see Fig 1). Do this on opposite edges, and on both ends of the wood.

2 Bore through all the mortises with the benchtop drill press and ¼ in. (6 mm) bit, and then use the mallet and bevel-edge chisels to pare the mortises to a smooth, true finish (see Fig 2). Work from both sides of the mortise to keep the edges clean. Don't damage the ends of the holes by levering the tool against the wood.

FIG 3

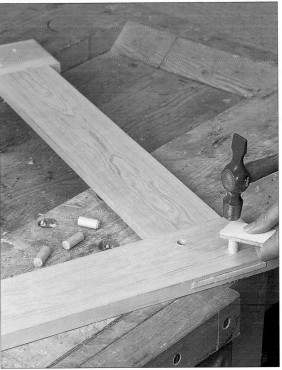

FIG 5

3 Use the square, marking knife and gauge to set out the 4 in.-(100 mm)-long tenons. Attach the router to its table, fit the ⅜ in. (10 mm) groove cutter in the router, set the fence to 4 in. (100 mm) and the depth of cut to ¼ in. (6 mm). Make a series of passes to cut away the waste (see Fig 3). Repeat this procedure on both sides and both ends, so that you finish up with ⁵⁄₁₆ in.-(8 mm)-thick tenons.

FIG 4

4 Reset the fence to ⅜ in. (10 mm) and run the rabbets for the mirror on the inside back edges of the frame. Put the frame components together and use the ½ in. (12 mm) bit to bore the dowel holes through the joints. Check for squareness and overall good fit (see Fig 4), and use the block plane to clean up the end grain.

5 Fit the frame together, drip glue into the drilled holes, and tap the dowels in with the hammer (see Fig 5). Leave the dowels standing above the front face of the frame. When the glue is completely dry, use the chisel to remove any from the surface and to trim the edges of the dowels to a slightly round-edged finish. Check that all rabbeted corners are free from glue. Use the graded sandpapers to rub the frame to a smooth finish. Finally, wipe away the dust, burnish the frame with the beeswax, fit the mirror glass and screw in the clips to hold it in place, and attach the screw eyes and the hanging wire.

TIP

To be certain that the mirror glass will fit the frame really well, it is best to take the frame to a glass store so it can be measured and the glass cut to fit exactly. Make sure that the glass is properly wrapped and protected before you leave the store.

Studio shelf system

This project covers that most basic of items—a simple shelf. For ease of making, it cannot be beat—there are no joints to cut, it is just made up of six boards and a handful of screws and dowels. The design is so well considered and cheap to make that you could easily put together a batch of units. Since the shelves are fixed directly to the wall with screws through the back boards, they can be removed easily and taken with you when you move. Simple to make and trouble free to fit—the perfect shelves!

Made of pine throughout, the construction is wonderfully straightforward. Instead of having the screws running into the end grain (which technically is a bad idea because the threads tend to pull out), they run down through pilot holes and into dowels set across the grain. The dowels are stained black, and the screwheads are covered with glued plugs. When you are driving the screws in, be careful not to over-tighten them to the extent that you expand the dowels and split the wood. Arrange the dowels so that the grain runs at right angles to the screw.

————— Essential Tools —————

workbench with vise and holdfast, compass, pencil, ruler, square, block plane, hammer, clamps, benchtop drill press, ½ in. (12 mm) twist bit, large bevel-edge knife, ¼ in. (7 mm) counter-bore bit with a plug cutter to match, screwdriver, sanding block, paintbrush

OTHER USEFUL TOOLS
cordless screwdriver, power sander, marking knife

Studio shelf system

6½ in.
(160 mm)

6½ in.
(160 mm)

¾ in.
(20 mm)

¼ in.
(7 mm) plug

10 in.
(250 mm)

1 in.
(25 mm)

38½ in.
(960 mm)

⅜ in.
(10 mm)

¾ in.
(20 mm)

6½ in.
(160 mm)

¾ in.
(20 mm)

If you like the design of the shelf system but would prefer not to use dowels, see the Adjustable Porch Chair on page 130 for an alternative method of fixing, using hex-head fasteners.

Materials

pine (see cutting list)

wood scraps for the drilling jig

6 nails for the jig: size to suit

8 in. (200 mm) length of ½ in. (12 mm) dowel

22 countersunk steel screws:
1¼ in. (30 mm) × no. 8

sandpaper grades 150 to 300

black felt-tip marker

PVA glue

oil-based matte varnish

mineral spirits to clean brush

Cutting List

all pieces cut from pine

2 pieces 38½ × 6½ × ¾ in.
(960 × 160 × 20 mm) (shelf boards)

2 pieces 10 × 6½ × ¾ in.
(250 × 160 × 20 mm) (end boards)

2 pieces 10 × 6½ × ¾ in.
(250 × 160 × 20 mm) (backboards)

You'll need to know

HAND PLANING
p.20

DRILLING HOLES
p.19

SCREWING
p.24

FIG 1

FIG 2

1 Take all six prepared boards (cut to size and planed) and check them over to make sure that they are in good condition, with no warps, splits or badly placed knots. Use the block plane to bring the ends to a good finish and to bevel all the edges slightly (see Fig 1).

2 Use the hammer, nails, and scraps to build a jig (a device for holding a component during construction) as a stop for one end of a shelf board. Put a shelf in the jig and clamp it to the table of the benchtop drill press so the ½ in. (12 mm) bit is in position. Bore out the dowel holes (see Fig 2).

FIG 3

FIG 5

3 Use a ruler and pencil to mark off ⅞ in. (23 mm) intervals on the ½ in. (12 mm) dowel. Set the knife on the mark, and roll the dowel to cut it through (see Fig 3). Note how the wide bevel on the knife gives the dowel a rounded end.

5 Use the counter-bore bit to drill holes through the end boards and backboards. Drive the screws in so that their heads are about ³⁄₁₆ in. (5 mm) below the surface (see Fig 5—shows backboard being screwed to shelf).

FIG 4

FIG 6

4 Sand the dowel ends to a slightly domed finish. Stain the ends with the marker (see Fig 4). Push the dowels into the holes in the ends of the shelves (they will stand slightly above the surface).

6 Cut plugs from a scrap of pine and glue them in place to cover the screws. Finally, sand the entire shelf system to a good finish and brush on a coat of varnish (see Fig 6).

Construction variations

A rabbet in the top piece can improve the appearance

Top piece overhangs the end of the shelf

Machine screw attaches top to sides

Screw socket

Plastic fastening blocks can be used on all the joints

Waste basket

This is the perfect basket for the design-conscious home. Get rid of your creaky woven baskets and plastic tubs left over from the 1970s—now you can have a basket that looks as if it belongs in the twenty-first century. This basket will also look good in a home office, or perhaps in a child's room.

Made of top-quality birch plywood throughout, this is one of the easiest projects in the book. The holes must be cut very carefully, and the five boards need to be prepared, glued, and nailed together, but apart from that, the construction is amazingly straightforward. The design is also very flexible, so you can choose to change the pattern of drilled holes, or go for a fretwork design rather than have holes, or paint the basket in a bright primary color instead of the natural finish. Do not be tempted to cut costs by using one of the soft-centered plywoods (those originating from Malaysia), because they are of inferior quality. You must use top-quality birch plywood. Ask your supplier for advice if you are not sure what to buy.

——————— Essential Tools ———————

workbench with vise, pencil, ruler, square, awl,
benchtop drill press, 1 in. (25 mm) and 1½ in. (40 mm)
forstner bits, clamps, power sander, hammer, sanding
block, paintbrush

OTHER USEFUL TOOLS
marking knife

Waste basket

Diagram labels:

12¼ in. (306 mm) 12¼ in. (306 mm)

18¾ in. (470 mm)

2 in. (50 mm)

1 in. (25 mm)

2¾ in. (70 mm)

1½ in. (40 mm)

2 in. (50 mm)

Note the way the sides follow each other so that you only see one edge on each side.

Materials

birch plywood (see cutting list)

masking tape

sandpaper grades 100 and 150

PVA glue

24 × ½ in. (12 mm) steel brads

teak oil

Cutting List

all pieces cut from birch plywood

4 pieces 18¾ × 12 × ¼ in.
(470 × 300 × 6 mm) (sides)

1 piece 11¾ × 11¾ × ½ in.
(294 × 294 × 12 mm) (base)

FIG 1

1 Take one of the side boards and use the ruler and square to draw out a 2 x 2 in. (50 x 50 mm) grid (see Fig 1). Double-check the measurements to make sure that the grid is accurate.

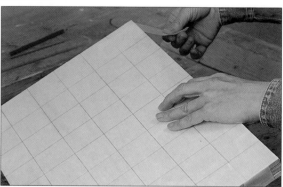

FIG 2

2 Take the four boards that make up the sides and sandwich them together, with the gridded board on top of the stack. Tape them together with masking tape (see Fig 2). Study our design, decide on the pattern of holes you want, and mark the center points with the awl.

FIG 3

3 Fit one or other of the forstner bits in the benchtop drill press, put a waste board on the drill table, and set to work boring the pattern of holes (see Fig 3). To ensure that each hole is cleanly worked, center the bit on the marked point, and then clamp the workpiece in place.

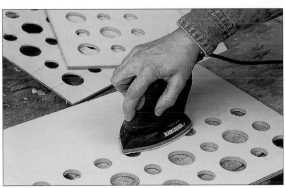

FIG 4

4 When you have bored all the holes, remove the masking tape, and use the sander to rub the surfaces to a smooth finish (see Fig 4). Be careful not to blur the edges.

FIG 5

5 Fold a piece of fine-grade sandpaper and use it to wipe around the cut edges of the drilled holes (see Fig 5). Continue until the edges are smooth to the touch.

FIG 6

6 Sand the edges of the baseboard and glue and nail the sides in place (see Fig 6). Don't let the brads run off course and split the plywood. Finally, sand the basket to a smooth finish and wipe on a coat of teak oil.

TIP

If you are worried about your ability to knock the brads into the edge of the thin plywood, then either ask a friend to help you align the brads, or drill pilot holes with a hand drill and a fine bit.

Construction variations

Lap-jointed corners glued and nailed

Plywood sides glued and nailed to corner pieces

Handle holes

Jointed frame with plywood sides glued into grooves

Half-lapped frame at the top and bottom glued and nailed to corner posts

Plywood sides glued and nailed to frame

Child's stool

This beautiful stool was inspired by a stool that my grandmother had in her country kitchen. When grandad had a few drops of paint left over from another job, the stool was painted. One time it was chicken coop red, and then garden gate green, but mostly—I don't know why—it was a vivid yellow. My grandparents used it as a footstool, for standing on to reach high cupboards, and for any number of other tasks, but mostly it was my own special seat. You too may find that the stool fulfills a number of roles.

Even if you are the newest of new weekend carpenters, you will be able to manage the construction process easily. Made from ¾ in.-(20 mm)-thick pine boards throughout, the components are cut out on the scroll saw. The splayed legs are housed in grooves cut on the inside face of the two apron boards, and the stool is held together with screws. We have painted it yellow, but other bright colors also work well, such as fire engine red or electric blue. You could also paint each part in a different color.

Essential Tools

workbench with vise and holdfast, compass,
pencil, ruler, square, bevel gauge, scroll saw, benchtop
drill press or electric drill, ⅜ in. (10 mm) and ³⁄₁₆ in.
(5 mm) twist bits, tenon saw, ⅝ in. (16 mm) bevel-edge
chisel, block plane, sanding block, countersink bit,
screwdriver, paintbrush

OTHER USEFUL TOOLS
cordless screwdriver, power sander, dividers,
marking knife

Child's stool

8 in.
(200 mm)

16 in.
(400 mm)

2⅜ in.
(60 mm)

15⅜ in.
(390 mm)

14³⁄₁₆ in.
(360 mm)

rounded
edges

4¾ in.
(120 mm)

3¼ in.
(80 mm)

3⅝ in.
(90 mm)

3⅝ in.
(90 mm)

3¼ in.
(80 mm)

The hole in the center of the seat (detail shown right), which doubles as a handle, must be small enough to ensure that a child cannot get a leg stuck in it.

Materials

pine (see cutting list)

sandpaper grades 80 and 150

12 countersunk steel screws:
1¼ in. (30 mm) × no. 8

gloss paint: yellow

mineral spirits to clean the brush

Cutting List

all pieces cut from pine

1 piece 16 × 8 × ¾ in.
(400 × 200 × 18 mm) (seat board)

2 pieces 15⅜ × 2⅜ × ¾ in.
(390 × 60 × 18 mm) (apron boards)

2 pieces 10½ × 10½ × ¾ in.
(260 × 260 × 18 mm) (leg boards)

4 in.
(100 mm)

1¾ in.
(45 mm)

FIG 1

FIG 2

1 Check the prepared boards for possible problems such as splits and badly placed knots. Use the square and bevel gauge to carefully lay out the design. When you come to the leg boards, start by drawing a centerline, and then use the line as a reference point for all the subsequent measurements (see Fig 1).

2 Use the scroll saw to cut out the component parts. Work at a steady, controlled pace, making sure that the line of cut is slightly to the waste side of the drawn line (see Fig 2). If you feel the blade running off course, or it sags, or the cut edge of the wood becomes brown and shiny, the blade probably needs replacing.

FIG 3

FIG 5

3 Drill a pilot hole through the seat with the ⅜ in. (10 mm) twist bit, pass one end of the scroll saw blade through the hole, refit the blade and tension it until it "pings." Cut along the marked line until the waste drops clear (see Fig 3).

5 Use the block plane to work all the exposed edges to a slightly rounded finish (as shown in Figs 4 and 6). With the chisel and sandpaper, adjust the sides of the leg boards so that they meet the apron boards for a tight push-fit (see Fig 5). Mark the parts with a pencil so that the joints are cut to a paired fit.

TIP

When using a chisel to cut a housing groove, make sure that the chisel is slightly narrower than the finished width of the groove.

FIG 4

FIG 6

4 To create the housing groove on the apron boards, make two cuts with the tenon saw [¾ in. (20 mm) slanting to 2³⁄₁₆ in. (60 mm) from the end; with a parallel ¹¹⁄₁₆ in. (18 mm) away, ³⁄₁₆ in. (5 mm) deep]. Clear the waste with the chisel (see Fig 4).

6 Drill pilot holes with the ³⁄₁₆ in. (5 mm) bit, followed by the countersink bit. Screw the apron boards to the legs and the seat board to the top edge of the aprons, countersinking all the screws. Rub with the finest grade of sandpaper, wipe up all the dust, and give the stool a coat of yellow gloss paint (see Fig 6). Repeat the procedure for a high-gloss finish.

Turned fruit bowl

Fruit always makes an attractive display while it is waiting to be eaten, particularly when it is contained in a beautiful bowl. Wooden bowls look especially appealing, and as a natural material, they complement the fruit perfectly. And what could be better than using a fruit bowl that you have made yourself? Just think of the kudos when your family and friends see the evidence of your talents—you can expect some orders for gifts.

There is no need to get involved in the expensive and tiresome business of searching around for a suitable block of wood. The good thing about this project is that the bowl is made from straight-grained American oak, and the blank (form for the bowl) is built up in laminated slices cut from a prepared board. The laminating procedure is a bit messy and time consuming, but on the other hand it means that you do not have to worry about loose knots or splits, or the wood warping out of shape.

───────── Essential Tools ─────────

workbench with vise, compass, pencil, ruler,
scroll saw, 4 long-reach sash or C-clamps, good-size
lathe with a 6 in.-(150 mm)-diameter face plate and
the capacity to turn a blank bigger than 10 in. (250
mm) in diameter, screwdriver, set of turning tools to
include a large gouge and a round-nosed scraper,
tailstock drill chuck to fit your lathe, full-face respirator
or dust mask and goggles, hearing protection,
2 in. (50 mm) forstner bit, sanding block

OTHER USEFUL TOOLS
cordless screwdriver, power sander, dividers

Turned fruit bowl

10 in.
(250 mm)

1 in.
(25 mm)

4⅝ in.
(115 mm)

1⅝ in.
(40 mm)

6¹⁄₁₆ in.
(155 mm)

While we use American oak throughout, you could substitute two different colored woods to achieve a counterbalanced color effect, for added interest.

*You'll need
to know*

CUTTING CURVES
p.18

WOODTURNING
p.25

NATURAL FINISHES
p.26

Materials

American oak (see cutting list)

PVA glue

countersunk steel screws to fit lathe face plate

sandpaper grades 100 to 300

vegetable oil

lint-free cotton cloth to apply the vegetable oil

Cutting List

all pieces cut from American oak

1 piece 10 × 10 × 1⅝ in.
(250 × 250 × 40 mm) (base slab)

3 pieces 10 × 10 × 1⅝ in.
(250 × 250 × 25 mm) (top slabs)

FIG 1

1 Take your planed wood and use the compass, set at a radius of 5 in. (125 mm), to lay out the four 10 in.-(250 mm)-diameter disks. Cut out the disks on the scroll saw (see Fig 1).

FIG 2

2 Smear a generous amount of PVA glue on mating surfaces, set the wood together in a stack, with all the edges more or less aligned, and clamp them (see Fig 2). Don't worry about the dripping glue. Leave for at least 24 hours and then remove the clamps.

FIG 3

3 Set the lathe face plate directly over the center point of the wood and attach with three or more steel screws (see Fig 3). It is important that the wood is centered and the whole thing is secure. Do not use soft brass or aluminium screws instead of steel, and do not be tempted to shorten the drying time for the glue in step 2.

FIG 4

FIG 6

4 Mount the whole thing on the lathe and set the tool rest just below the center of spin (see Fig 4). Rotate the wood blank by hand to make sure that the tool rest is clear.

6 Remove the tool rest and fit the 2 in. (50 mm) forstner bit in the tailstock chuck. Slowly advance the tailstock to bore a pilot hole to a depth of about 3⅝ in. (90 mm), so that it stops about 1 in. (25 mm) short of the bowl bottom (see Fig 6). Keep withdrawing the bit to remove the waste.

TIP

Woodturning is potentially dangerous. Put on protective gear and ensure that clothing does not present a hazard.

FIG 5

FIG 7

5 First, use the large gouge to turn the wood to a smooth cylinder 10 in. (250 mm) in diameter, and then turn the cylinder to the shape of the outside of the bowl (see Fig 5). Keep resetting the rest so that it is near the workpiece.

7 Move the tool rest so that it is over the bed and very cautiously use the gouge, followed by the scraper, to turn out the center of the bowl (see Fig 7). Work until you reach the bottom of the drilled pilot hole. When you are pleased with the profile, rub the bowl with sandpaper and burnish it with vegetable oil.

Kitchen cutting boards

It is really good to see family and friends using small items that I have made with my own two hands. One day I was looking at a couple of pieces of apple wood and wondering what to make with them, and came up with the idea of kitchen cutting boards. Not so long afterward, the boards were out on the table being used for cutting bread and cheese. These boards are not particularly special, in fact they are rather humble, but the warm feeling I get when I see them in use is due to the pleasure of making them, and the knowledge that they are going to be of service for years to come.

Both boards are made from apple wood turned on the lathe. One is decorated by pyrography (branding with a hot iron), while the other is chip carved. Pyrography is very easy: you simply heat the iron and press it into the wood. The chip-carved design is just as straightforward—lots of little boat-shaped knife cuts make a stylized sheaf of wheat design that is really appropriate for a breadboard. Practice the technique on scrap wood first.

Essential Tools

workbench with vise and holdfast, compass, pencil, ruler, scroll saw, lathe with a bowl-turning option and a large face plate, set of turning tools to include a skew chisel, gouge and a round-nosed scraper, full-face respirator or dust mask and goggles, hearing protection, sanding block, dividers, electric soldering iron, small penknife

OTHER USEFUL TOOLS
selection of knives

Kitchen cutting boards

⁵⁄₃₂ in.- (10 mm)- wide bands of decoration

⁵⁄₃₂ in.- (10 mm)-wide bands of decoration

1¼ in. (30 mm) 1¼ in. (30 mm) 12 in. (300 mm) ⅝ in. (15 mm)

12 in. (300 mm) 1¼ in. (30 mm)

Materials

apple wood (see cutting list)

countersunk steel screws to fit lathe face plate

sandpaper grades 100 to 300

olive oil and lint-free cotton cloth to apply it

Cutting List

2 pieces apple wood 12 × 12 × 1¼ in.
(300 × 300 × 30 mm) (boards)

While apple wood has been used for both these boards (because the texture and color improve with age), you could replace it with just about any fruit wood instead, such as pear, cherry, or plum. Avoid exotic woods that leach sap or woods that smell when they are wet.

PYROGRAPHY BOARD

FIG 1

1 Check the slab of wood to make sure that it is absolutely sound throughout, with no knots or splits. Make a point of taking a really close look at the end grain, because there is nothing quite so disappointing as going to all the trouble of turning and decorating, only to see the board split in half. Look at the two faces of the board to see which is best. Set your compass to the largest radius that can be accommodated on the board, and draw a circle on the poorer face (see Fig 1). Mark the center point with a cross, making sure that it is clearly visible.

FIG 2

2 Prepare the circle for the carved board at the same time as the pyrography board. Fit the scroll saw with a large-toothed blade and adjust the tension so that the blade "pings" when plucked. Cut out the two disks (see Fig 2). These are the blanks for the boards.

FIG 3

FIG 4

3 Set the lathe face plate flat on one of the blanks and align it so that the drawn cross is accurately centered. Clamp the blank to the bench with the holdfast and attach the face plate to the wood with three or more screws (see Fig 3). Mount the face plate securely on the lathe.

4 Adjust the tool rest so that it is just below the center of spin. Put on your dust mask, goggles, and hearing protection, and roll up your sleeves. Turn on the power and use the gouge to turn the wood to a smooth disk. Use the skew chisel to turn a slope around the edge (see Fig 4).

FIG 5

FIG 6

5 When you have cut a precise disk, take a fold of medium-grade sandpaper and rub the surface to a smooth finish. Set the dividers to ⅜ in. (10 mm) and use them to scribe a series of step-offs around the border (see Fig 5). Scribe as many step-offs as you want to decorate.

6 Remove the board from the face plate. Turn on the soldering iron and wait until it is red-hot. Practice on some scrap wood to create a design that you like. Burn the design into the board (see Fig 6). Finally, give it a rub down with olive oil.

CARVED BOARD

FIG 1

FIG 2

7 Mount the sawed blank on the lathe as described in step 3 for the pyrography board. Turn it to a smooth disk, and then with the skew chisel, round over the edge of the disk so that it is nicely convex in cross-section (see Fig 1). Use sandpaper to clean up the edge and rub the raised center to a good finish.

8 Continue shaping the edge of the disk until you have a border about 2 in. (50 mm) wide. Set the dividers to ⅜ in. (10 mm) and cut three step-offs around the center of the border. Take the round-nosed scraper and sculpt a groove on the innermost edge of the border (see Fig 2). Remove the disk from the lathe and sand the back.

FIG 3

9 Put the disk on the bench. With the small penknife, work around the outer border cutting a series of stop-cuts — cuts that run to a depth of about ⅛ in. (3 mm). Run a second series of cuts alongside the first to remove boat-shaped chips of wood and create little pockets (see Fig 3).

FIG 4

10 Repeat the chip-cutting procedure as described, only this time work in the opposite direction so that the chips form a chevron, like a stylized sheaf of wheat (see Fig 4). Brush away the dust and debris, check that the back is smooth, give the wood a coat of olive oil, and the board is ready to use.

Construction variations

Angled edge   V-shaped grooves

Rounded edge   U-shaped grooves

A recess for a round ceramic tile

A wide border for carved or burnt decoration

TV and video table

The idea for this project came to me when I was watching television and suddenly realized that the whole television setup was a mess. Not only was the video recorder sitting on the floor, with the videotapes piled high on a side chair, but worse still, cables and wires snaked all over the place. I decided it would be much neater to have one table fitted snugly in the corner housing all the equipment and hiding the wires.

Apart from a couple of dowels, the table is made from birch plywood throughout, and has four swivel wheels on the underside. Its triangular shape allows it to fit into the corner of a room. The idea is that the television sits on the top surface, the video recorder slides on one shelf, videotapes and magazines are stored on the other, and the cables run out of the back corner of the table directly to the sockets. With the surfaces left natural and wiped over with oil, the table is functional, modern and attractive.

If you like the overall idea of the project, but would prefer to have four shelves, or you want to include a rack for videotapes, the design is flexible enough to allow for modifications and you can adapt it to suit your needs.

―――――――― Essential Tools ――――――――

workbench with vise and holdfast, pencil,
ruler, compass, square, block plane, sanding
block, jigsaw, electric drill, ½ in. (12 mm) forstner bit,
¼ in. (7 mm) counter-bore bit with a plug cutter to
match, screwdriver, awl, paintbrush

OTHER USEFUL TOOLS
cordless screwdriver, power sander, marking knife

TV and video table

31½ in.
(790 mm)

36 in. (90 mm) radius

28 in.
(700 mm)

The dowels pass through the middle shelf and are held between the top and bottom boards. They help support the weight of the television.

10 in.
(250 mm)

½ in.
(12 mm) dowel

You'll need to know

CUTTING CURVES
p.18

SCREWING
p.24

NATURAL FINISHES
p.26

Materials

birch plywood and pine (see cutting list)

sandpaper grade 100

PVA glue

12 countersunk steel screws: ¾ in. (20 mm) × no. 8

6 white plastic joining blocks with screws to fit

teak oil

4 swivel wheels with screws to fit

Cutting List

2 isosceles triangles of birch plywood cut from a square 31½ × 31½ × ½ in. (790 × 790 × 12 mm) (top and bottom boards)

1 isosceles triangle of birch plywood cut from a square 31⅛ × 31⅛ × ½ in. (778 × 778 × 12 mm) (middle shelf)

2 pieces of birch plywood 28 × 10½ × ½ in. (700 × 250 × 12 mm) (side boards)

2 × 10⅜ in. (260 mm) lengths of ½ in. (12 mm) pine dowel

FIG 1

will be the side edges (this indicates where the edge of the side board underneath is). Set the compass to 36 in. (90 mm), set on the right-angled corner of the triangle and draw a quarter-circle (see Fig 1). Do this on all three boards.

FIG 2

1 Take the top and bottom boards, and the middle shelf, and clean up the edges with the block plane and sandpaper. Make sure that the top and bottom boards are absolutely identical in size. With the pencil, rule a ½ in. (12 mm) border on the face of the top and bottom boards, on what

2 Use the holdfast to secure the workpiece to the bench—so that the right-angled corner is well clear—and then take the jigsaw and cut out the corner detail (see Fig 2). Repeat this procedure on all three boards.

FIG 3

3 Drill the dowel holes with the ½ in. (12 mm) bit. The holes go right through the middle shelf and only half-way through the inside face of the top and bottom boards. Drill holes for the screws with the ¼ in. (7 mm) counter-bore bit. Glue and screw the top board to the side boards. Cut plugs and glue them over the screwheads. Attach the middle shelf with the plastic joining blocks (see Fig 3).

FIG 4

4 Slide the two ½ in. (12 mm) dowels into place, and drill, glue, and screw the bottom board into position (see Fig 4). Plug the screws as for the top board. Rub everything with the graded sandpapers and apply some teak oil.

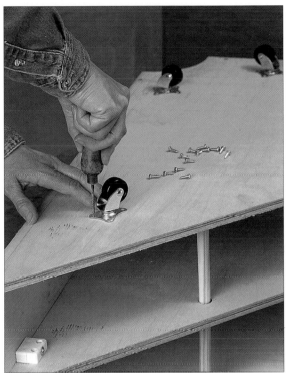

FIG 5

5 Turn the table over so that the underside of the bottom board is uppermost and mark the position of the four swivel wheels. Make holes with the awl and screw the wheels in place (see Fig 5). Finally, give the top surface another rub-down with the finest grade of sandpaper, followed by another coat of teak oil. Oil the whole table several more times over the next 48 hours.

TIP

If you like the idea of the project but want to cut costs and go for a more basic structure, you could use faced particleboard instead of plywood, and leave out the glue and screws and use the plastic fastening blocks throughout.

Studio table

Designed to complement the Adjustable Porch Chair on pages 130–135, this table is an absolute classic—a truly beautiful piece of quality modern furniture, a piece that draws its inspiration from medieval trestle tables.

Made from American oak throughout, this table looks equally at home in the studio or dining room. The secret of its appeal is the choice of wood, the generous width and thickness of the boards, and the simplicity of the design. The great thing about the table is that it can be made without cutting any joints: the boards are simply butted or sandwiched and then fitted with hex-head bolts that run through the thickness of the wood. The two X-frames that make up the legs are linked by the tabletop and the under-stretchers in such a way that the whole structure becomes stable. To finish the surface, the wood is wire-brushed to give it a weathered texture and then wiped with Danish oil. If you like this design but are put off by the price of American oak, the alternative is not to reduce costs by buying thinner boards, but to opt for pine instead and slightly increase the thickness of the boards you purchase.

Essential Tools

workbench with vise, compass, pencil, ruler, square, bevel gauge, clamps, benchtop drill press, ⅜ in. (10 mm) forstner bit, ³⁄₁₆ in. (5 mm) twist bit, crosscut saw, block plane, wire brush, sanding block, paintbrush, countersink bit, electric drill, a screwdriver bit, hacksaw, metal file, allen key to fit the hex-heads, screwdriver

OTHER USEFUL TOOLS
power sander

Studio table

10 in.
(250 mm)

Cross-table board

70 in.
(1750 mm)

Approximate
screw position

Stretcher board

Bolt

5¾ in.
(145 mm)

5¾ in.
(145 mm)

3³⁄₁₆ in.
(80 mm)

42 in.
(1050 mm)

4¹³⁄₁₆ in.
(120 mm)

15³⁄₁₆ in.
(380 mm)

The dimensions of this table and the position of the legs make it suitable for seating six people—one at each end and two on each side.

Materials

American oak (see cutting list)

sandpaper grades 100 to 300

Danish oil

20 countersunk steel screws:
1½ in. (35 mm) × no. 8

4 bolts: steel and
brass hex-head fasteners
complete with threaded
steel rod to fit

8 countersunk steel screws:
3 in. (75 mm) × no. 8

Cutting List

all pieces cut from American oak

4 pieces 36¾ × 5¾ × ⅞ in.
(920 × 145 × 22 mm) (leg boards)

3 pieces 70 × 10 × ⅞ in.
(1750 × 250 × 22 mm)
(tabletop boards)

2 pieces 30¼ × 5¾ × ⅞ in.
(755 × 145 × 22 mm)
(cross-table boards)

2 pieces 42 × 5¾ × ⅞ in.
(1050 × 145 × 22 mm)
(stretcher boards)

2 pieces 5¾ × 1 × ⅞ in.
(145 × 25 × 22 mm)
(distance blocks)

*You'll need
to know*

**DRILLING HOLES
p.19**

**SPECIAL FINISHES
p.27**

**SCREWING
p.24**

FIG 1

FIG 2

1 Take the four 36¾ in. (920 mm) leg boards, measure 4 in. (100 mm) along from each end, and use the bevel gauge to run a line across from the 4 in. (100 mm) mark to the corner (see Fig 1).

2 Set the leg boards together to form the X-frames and clamp. Mark the positions of the screw and bolt holes. Drill the holes ³⁄₁₆ in. (5 mm) for the screws and ⅜ in. (10 mm) for the bolts (see Fig 2).

FIG 3

FIG 5

3 Use the crosscut saw to cut the leg boards to shape. Plane the end grain to a good finish. Use the wire brush to scour out the soft part of the grain, so that the surface feels rough to the touch (see Fig 3). Sand lightly. Give all the boards a couple of coats of Danish oil.

5 Cut the threaded rod to length with the hacksaw (to suit the brass hex-heads) and file the ends so that they run smoothly into the hex-heads. Slide the rods through the X-frame leg boards, thread on the hex-heads, and tighten them with the allen key (see Fig 5).

FIG 4

FIG 6

4 Set the three 10 in.-(250 mm)-wide tabletop boards face down on the workbench with ⅝ in.-(15 mm)-thick spacers of scrap wood to keep them apart. Place the two cross-table boards in position, and check with the square to make sure the angle between the legs and the table surface is 90°. Drill holes with the countersink bit and screw them in place using the screwdriver attachment on the drill. Use two 1½ in. (35 mm) screws for each crossover of the two boards (see Fig 4). The two cross-table boards should be 42 in. (1072 mm) apart.

6 Butt the X-frame leg boards against the cross-table board, fit and clamp one of the spacer blocks and fix with 3 in. (75 mm) screws (see Fig 6). Do this at both ends of the table. Finally, set the stretcher boards in place, on what will be the underside of the X-frame legs, and screw them in position with 1½ in. (35 mm) screws.

Turned table lamp

The design of this lamp evolved after considering the technical problems of making a turned lamp with a flex hole down its center, without using a single piece of expensive wood. The lamp can be used in any room if you fit an appropriate shade. The shape of the form can also be modified to suit your tastes, and the size and power of your lathe.

The lamp base is made from pine throughout. Four small square sections are each planed along one arris (sharp edge) and then glued together in such a way that the four cut-away corners form the flex hole. While the form is still on the lathe, it is stained with a felt-tip pen and burnished with wax. This is a nice, straightforward project if you are new to woodturning—it's inexpensive and there is no need to drill a deep hole for the lamp flex. Although I used a pen for staining the wood, you could also use a oil-based wood dye, or even a water based wood dye followed by a coat of varnish. This lamp is made from four sections, however if anyone offers you a single chunk of seasoned pine, don't turn it down.

Essential Tools

workbench with vise, compass, pencil, ruler, smoothing plane, 4 short sash clamps, benchtop drill press, 2 in. (50 mm) forstner bit, good-size lathe with an expanding chuck and the capacity to turn a blank bigger than 10 in. (250 mm) in diameter, set of turning tools to include a large gouge, a skew chisel and a round-nosed scraper, full-face respirator or dust mask and goggles, hearing protectors, screwdriver

OTHER USEFUL TOOLS
cordless screwdriver, power sander

Turned table lamp

1⅝ in.
(40 mm)

8 in.
(200 mm)

8 in.
(200 mm)

Make sure that the four pine sections you buy are properly seasoned, otherwise the turned form will shrink and split.

Materials

pine (see cutting list)

PVA glue

sandpaper grades 100 to 150

a couple of permanent black felt-tip markers

beeswax polish

lint-free cotton cloth to apply the beeswax

lamp head complete with flex,
plug and screws to fit

lampshade to suit

Cutting List

4 pieces pine 8 × 4 × 4 in. (200 × 100 × 100 mm)

TIP

Woodturning is potentially dangerous, so be very aware of safety. Always make sure you are suitably dressed, with no dangling hair or jewelry, and no flapping cuffs. Always wear a dust mask and goggles, or a full-face respirator mask; hearing protection is also recommended. Keep children away.

FIG 1

1 Take the four 8 in.-(200 mm)-long pine sections and group them four-square so that the best faces are outermost. Plane back the central corners ⅜ in. (10 mm) (see Fig 1).

FIG 2

2 Regroup the blocks, clamping them together in a trial run to ensure that the mating faces come together tight and flush. If necessary, use the plane to cut back the faces. Take the stack apart. Then spread PVA glue on the mating faces of two neighboring blocks and clamp them (see Fig 2). Repeat this procedure with the other two blocks. When the glue is dry, glue and clamp the paired blocks to make the single four-block blank with a small central hole.

FIG 3

FIG 5

3 Tap a stick of scrap in each end of the central hole. Use the 2 in. (50 mm) forstner bit to bore to a depth of about ⅜ in. (10 mm) in one end of the block. Mount the blank on the expanding chuck and draw up the tailstock center (see Fig 3). Rotate the wood by hand to test all is correct.

5 Use the gouge to turn the cylinder into a rough cone shape (the base of the cone is nearest to the expanding chuck). Change over to the round-nosed scraper and skew chisel and continue turning until the lines of the cone are clean and smooth (see Fig 5).

FIG 4

FIG 6

4 Arrange the tool rest so that it is clear of the workpiece. Put on the protective gear, roll up your sleeves, and tie back your hair. Use the large gouge to turn the square section into the largest possible cylinder (see Fig 4). Use the skew chisel to skim the wood to a smooth finish. Tighten up the tailstock center.

6 Take the felt-tip pen and run it up and down the spinning cone until the surface is completely black (see Fig 6). Do this several times to ensure even coverage. Use the sandpaper and beeswax to burnish the surface to a high gloss finish. Screw-fit the lamp socket to the top of the cone, join up the flex and attach the shade.

Bathroom cabinet

The design for this project, like many designs, grew and evolved. When we are planning projects, we often sit around with pencil, paper, and a cup of tea, and figure out the options. In this instance, I started out with an idea for no more than a towel rail. Then Gill suggested that we have a rail with a shelf. I thought that we might as well have a couple of shelves. Gill volunteered that perhaps we ought to add two doors, with attractive hinges and tiny knobs—so it went on. Before long we finished up with a project for a little cupboard complete with a rail, two doors, a carved turnbuckle, two whittled knobs, and routed details.

The cabinet is mainly made from laminated pine. The two shelves are housed in the end boards, while the three vertical posts are dowelled into the shelves, and the rail is held between the end boards. To finish the cabinet, it is rubbed with graded sandpapers and wiped with teak oil.

Essential Tools

workbench with vise and holdfast, compass, pencil, ruler, square, tracing paper, scroll saw, router and router table, ³⁄₁₆ and ½ in. (4 mm and 13 mm) groove cutters, cove cutter, 2 long sash clamps, benchtop drill press, ⅝ in. (15 mm) forstner bit, electric drill, ¼ in. (6 mm) twist bit, ¼ in. (6 mm) dowel marker studs, mallet, penknife, screwdriver, sanding block, paintbrush

OTHER USEFUL TOOLS
cordless screwdriver, power sander, dividers, marking knife

Bathroom cabinet

19½ in. (496 mm)

7½ in. (190 mm)

7½ in. (190 mm)

16 in. (400 mm)

1⅛ in. (30 mm)

7¾ in. (194 mm)

¾ in. (18 mm)

¾ in. (18 mm)

⅝ in. (15 mm) dowel

Materials

pine and plywood (see cutting list)

guide strip of waste wood: 14 in. (350 mm) long

12 × ¼ in. (30 mm) fixing dowels, ¼ in. (6 mm) in diameter

PVA glue

1 brass dome-headed screw: 1¼ in. (30 mm) × no. 8

sandpaper grades 100 to 150

4 decorative brass hinges with brass screws to fit: size and design to suit

teak oil

Cutting List

2 pieces pine 16 × 6 × ¾ in.
(400 × 150 × 18 mm) (end boards)

2 pieces pine 19 × 5 × ¾ in.
(476 × 126 × 18 mm) (shelf boards)

1 piece plywood 19 × 8⅜ × ³⁄₁₆ in.
(476 × 210 × 4 mm) (backboard)

3 pieces pine 7¾ × 1¼ × ¾ in.
(194 × 30 × 18 mm) (vertical battens)

19 in. (476 mm) length of ⅝ in. (15 mm) pine dowel (rail)

2 pieces pine 7½ × 7½ × ¾ in. (190 × 190 × 18 mm) (doors)

The length of the vertical battens allows for slightly loose-fitting doors, to avoid problems if the wood gets damp and expands. The template below is for half of an end board.

6 in. (150 mm)

8 in. (200 mm)

FIG 1

1 Take the 6 in.-(150 mm)-wide end boards and use the pencil, square, ruler, and tracing paper to carefully lay out all the lines that go to make up the design (see Fig 1). Although we have specified 6 in.-(150 mm)-wide boards at 16 in. (400 mm) long, if you can get the design out of boards left over from another project, that is fine. In this project we have actually used a wider piece of wood flawed by a couple of badly placed knots.

FIG 3

FIG 2

2 Label the best faces of the two end boards and then cut out the marked design on the scroll saw (see Fig 2). Work slowly, feeding the wood forward so that the blade is presented with the line of next cut. If you feel the blade pulling or the workpiece going off course, ease back and realign the cut. If the going gets heavy, switch off the power and check the blade. Maybe the blade needs changing or re-tensioning, or alternatively, perhaps the wood is damp.

3 Fit the ½ in. (13 mm) groove cutter in the router and attach the router to its table. Set one of the end boards flat on the bench, with the inside facing up, and clamp it into position. Clamp the guide strip across the board so that the router is able to run alongside it, with the cutter centered on the marked housing groove. Plunge the router forward and cut the groove. Make several passes to end up with a depth of ¾ in. (18 mm). Repeat this procedure for all four housings. With the benchtop drill press and the ⅝ in. (15 mm) bit, drill the rail holes to a depth of about ⁵⁄₁₆ in. (8 mm).

When you are ready to cut the cove detail on the shelf ends and edges, fit the cove cutter in the router, and move the fence back out of the way. Switch on the power, wait until the bit is running at full speed, and follow the bearing guide to make the cut (see Fig 3). If you are new to the procedure, make a trial run on some scrap wood.

FIG 4

4 Fit the ³⁄₁₆ in. (5 mm) groove cutter in the router, slide the fence up to ³⁄₁₆ in. (5 mm) and run a groove along the back edge of the side boards and the inner faces of the two shelves. Take the two shelves, establish the position of the three vertical battens (for the doors to hang on and for the middle post) and use the ¼ in. (6 mm) twist bit to drill the holes for the fixing dowels. Finally, fit the ½ in. (13 mm) groove cutter in the router, and run a shoulder ½ in. (13 mm) wide and ⅛ in. (3 mm) deep on the ends of the two shelves and the faces that will be the outside of the cupboard (see Fig 4).

FIG 5

5 Use the dowel marker studs to transfer the dowel positions from the shelf through to the ends of the vertical battens. The middle batten is pivoted so that it presents the ¾ in. (18 mm) thickness. Sink the holes with the ¼ in. (6 mm) twist bit to a depth of 1 in. (25 mm) (see Fig 5). Push the fixing dowels in. Use a small wrap of masking tape around the twist bit to act as a depth guide when drilling. Lightly sand the holes with a twist of sandpaper, until the dowels are a good push-fit.

FIG 6

6 Make a trial dry run to make sure that all the component parts come together well. When you are pleased with the results, spread glue in the housing grooves and in the dowel holes, use the mallet to put everything together, and clamp them (see Fig 6).

With the penknife, whittle the turnbuckle from scrap wood and screw it to the middle post. Note the little dowel that runs through the thickness of the central post to act as a stop for the two doors. Adjust the turnbuckle screw so that the buckle is gripped but not crushed.

FIG 7

7 Remove the clamps and sand all the surfaces to a good finish. Make sure that the rail is free to move in its end holes, and the back board is a loose, easy fit. Take a couple of pieces of scrap left over from the end boards, and whittle them into knobs with the penknife (see Fig 7). You can follow our stalk-like design or cut them to suit yourself—perhaps two little round shapes. If you are new to whittling or it is something that you would prefer not to do, you could fit store-bought handles or knobs. Drill holes for the knobs and glue them in place on the two doors.

Sand the edges of the doors to a good fit and use your chosen hinges to hang them on the doorposts. Rub all the surfaces to a smooth finish—especially the leading edges of the two side boards, and the edges of the doors. Wipe away the dust and apply a coat of teak oil. Finally, give the cabinet another sanding with the finest grade of sandpaper, remove the dust and complete the process with a further coat of teak oil.

TIP

If you are in any way worried about a procedure, it's always a good idea to make a trial run on some scrap wood first. Many woodworkers consider that their first effort is a trial run for the real thing. We did this too, making two cabinets—one as a prototype and one as the finished item.

Construction variations

Detail of the door construction for the design shown on the left

Alternative designs for handles

Butt hinges recessed into door frame

Alternative design with just one door, which is a frame and panel construction

Alternative design with plywood doors that have mirrors attached to the fronts

Towel rack

The goal of this project was to make a contemporary towel rack containing traditional elements, but which was not a copy of a historical original. It had to look modern, and yet, in spirit at least, it had to be a rustic piece. The design needed to be suitable for a beginner with the minimum of tools. As you can see, while this towel rack has many of the elements that you would expect to see on a classic rustic piece—pierced ends, rounded tops, handle holes, arched foot, and an ornate bottom rail—these are no more than stylized interpretations, achieved with the minimum of tools.

The whole thing is made from pine, with the end boards cut out on the scroll saw, and the bottom rail cut and then shaped with the spokeshave. All four rails are wedge-tenoned into the end boards. The wood is left in its natural state. It is a very easy item to make—the perfect project for a long weekend. If you like the idea of making a rustic design and yet do not feel up to turning complex rails on a lathe, this project is for you.

Essential Tools

workbench with vise and holdfast, compass, pencil, ruler, square, benchtop drill press, ½ in. (12 mm) and 2⅛ in. (55 mm) forstner bits, scroll saw, 2 long sash clamps, ½ in. (12 mm) and ¾ in. (20 mm) bevel-edge chisels, router and router table, ⅜ in. (10 mm) groove cutter, spokeshave, sanding block, penknife

OTHER USEFUL TOOLS
cordless screwdriver, power sander, electric drill, dividers, marking knife

Towel rack

6 in.
(150 mm) radius

2⅛ in.
(55 mm) hole

4⅝ in.
(115 mm)

1¼ in.
(30 mm)

4¾ in.
(120 mm)

36 in.
(900 mm)

4 in.
(100 mm)

3¼ in.
(80 mm)

4 in.
(100 mm)

3 in.
(75 mm) radius

30 in.
(750 mm)

9 in.
(225 mm)

*You'll need
to know*

DRILLING HOLES
p.19

**CUTTING CURVED
SHAPES**
p.18

ROUTING A TENON
p.21

Materials

pine (see cutting list)
sandpaper grades 100 and 120
PVA glue

Cutting List

all pieces cut from pine

2 pieces 36 × 9 × ¾ in.
(900 × 225 × 18 mm) (end boards)

3 pieces 30 × 1¼ × ¾ in.
(750 × 30 × 18 mm) (top rails)

1 piece 30 × 4 × ¾ in.
(750 × 100 × 18 mm) (bottom rail)

*This towel rack could also be used
as a display stand. Quilts, attractive
linens, patchwork, and embroidery
are good candidates for displaying
informally in this manner.*

FIG 1

FIG 2

1 Draw in centerlines on the end boards. Set the compass to a radius of 3 in. (75 mm) and trace the top and bottom details. Use the ruler to link up the details (see Fig 1).

2 Bore the handle hole with the 2⅛ in. (55 mm) forstner bit and cut out the form on the scroll saw. Cut in from both ends of the wood to meet at the middle (see Fig 2).

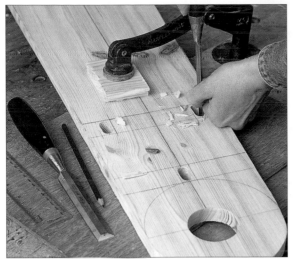

FIG 3

3 Drill the ends of the mortise holes with the ½ in. (12 mm) forstner bit. Clamp the work-piece flat on the bench and chop out the remaining waste with the ½ in. (12 mm) bevel-edge chisel (see Fig 3). Work from both sides so that the wood is not damaged when the chisel exits.

FIG 5

5 Cut out the shape of the bottom rail on the scroll saw and then use the spokeshave to bring the sawed edge to a rounded, smoothly curved finish (see Fig 5). Use the spoke-shave to chamfer the edges of the three top rails. Sand all the edges and faces to a smooth finish.

FIG 4

4 Fit the ⅜ in. (10 mm) groove cutter in the router and attach the router to its table. Draw the fence back, and set the bit to a height of ⅛ in. (3 mm). Pass the rails through the router and cut shoulders on both side faces. Reduce the bit height to ¹⁄₁₆ in. (1.5 mm) and cut shoulders on the top and bottom edge faces (see Fig 4).

FIG 6

6 With the penknife and chisels, carefully shape the square ends of the rails to fit the round-ended mortises (see Fig 6). When you have achieved a push-fit, run two saw kerfs (cuts) into the ends of the tenons. Finally, glue and wedge the rails in place, and sand the towel rack to a smooth finish, especially the top of the rails.

Sauna bench

This stylish seat is suitable for a bathroom or sauna, because it resists steam and hot water. Glue has not been used in its construction. It has been designed so that it can be built in the space of a day with the minimum of tools and expertise—there are no joints to make and there is no need for expensive tools. Material costs are low—we have opted for pine instead of using expensive endangered species such as mahogany, and the bench is put together without expensive brass or stainless-steel fittings.

After drawing lots of sketches and playing around with pieces of cardboard and scrap wood, we came up with this novel design. It's wonderfully simple—all the components are made from pine boards, and the bench is held together with four threaded rods complete with nuts, washers, and screws. We kept costs down by using zinc-plated rods, however you could improve on the quality of the finish by using stainless steel. Note how the inclusion of two stretcher pieces set into the top of the seat acts as an anti-wracking device (stops it from twisting) and keeps the structure square.

Essential Tools

workbench with vise and holdfast, pencil, ruler, square, benchtop drill press, ¼ in. (6 mm) twist bit, block plane, sanding block, clamps, screwdriver, pair of wrenches to fit the nuts, hacksaw, file

OTHER USEFUL TOOLS
cordless screwdriver, power sander

Sauna bench

seat stretchers

28 in.
(700 mm)

4 in.
(100 mm)

18⅛ in.
(460 mm)

4 in.
(100 mm)

15 in.
(380 mm)

4 in.
(100 mm)

**You'll need
to know**

**DRILLING HOLES
p.19**

**HAND PLANING
p.20**

**SCREWING
p.24**

Materials

pine (see cutting list)

sandpaper grades 100
and 120

4 countersunk steel screws:
1¼ in. (30 mm) × no. 8

4 × 16 in. (400 mm) lengths
of plated ¼ in. (6 mm)
threaded rod with 8 nuts and
8 washers to fit

Cutting List

all pieces cut from pine

20 pieces 28 × 2 × ¾ in.
(700 × 50 × 20 mm)
(seat and undershelf)

18 pieces 18⅛ × 2 × ¾ in.
(460 × 50 × 20 mm) (legs)

2 pieces 16 × 2 × ¾ in.
(400 × 50 × 20 mm)
(seat stretchers)

*The dimensions given are for a single-seat bench, but you could
double the length of the seat and undershelf pieces so that the
bench is long enough to stretch out on.*

FIG 1

TIP

**The jig ensures that holes can be
drilled accurately. Run the drill in and
out repeatedly, in order to clear the
waste from the hole, and to allow the
bit to cool down. Brush the debris off
the jig after each boring.**

1 Mark the position of the holes for the
threaded rod—see the working drawing—
and build a jig from scrap wood. Clamp the
jig to the table of the benchtop drill press and use
the ¼ in. (6 mm) bit to bore the holes (see Fig 1).

FIG 2

2 Use the block plane and the medium-grade sandpaper to remove the sharp edges from all 40 component parts (see Fig 2).

FIG 3

3 Clamp and screw the first seat stretcher in place and start sliding the components on to the threaded rods (see Fig 3). Be careful not to damage the thread or split the wood.

FIG 4

4 Ease each piece down the threaded rods, making sure the best edges form the upper surface of the seat (see Fig 4).

FIG 5

5 When you have screwed the other stretcher in place, and fitted the last two seat and undershelf pieces, use the square to ensure that the whole structure is true. Finally, tighten the nuts with the wrenches (see Fig 5), saw the ends off the threaded rods with the hacksaw and file them to a smooth finish.

Construction variations

Dovetail joint for joining the legs to the rails

Bridle joint for joining the legs to the rails

Halved joint for joining the legs to the rails

Brace

Spacers with drilled holes to take fixing rod

Only four legs of thicker section needed

Garden trug

This pretty garden trug or basket is reminiscent of the beautiful split wood baskets that were popular in Edwardian times. Prints of the period depicting garden scenes often show the lady of the house gliding around the garden with a parasol in one hand and a trug in the other. A trug is perfectly suited to carrying small tools and garden produce. You might use it when weeding a border, or when cutting flowers. Trugs are also suitable for indoor use— their design makes them ideal as a feature in the kitchen, perhaps for holding cutlery or bread, or even for decorative use as a table centerpiece.

The trug is made from pine throughout. The two side boards are worked on the scroll saw, the slats are pinned in place, the shaped uprights are screwed to the side boards, and the handle is simply held between the supports. A unique feature of this design is the whittled stretcher handle, which has a curved form and dappled texture. To finish, it was colorwashed with acrylic paint, followed by a couple of coats of teak oil.

─────────── Essential Tools ───────────

workbench with vise and holdfast, pencil, ruler,
compass, square, bevel gauge, clamp, jigsaw, benchtop
drill press, ⅝ in. (15 mm) forstner bit, scroll saw,
hammer, screwdriver, knife, block plane,
sanding block, 2 paintbrushes

OTHER USEFUL TOOLS
cordless screwdriver, power sander, electric drill,
marking knife, bandsaw

Garden trug

17⅜ in.
(440 mm)

⅝ in.
(15 mm) hole

8 in.
(200 mm)

⅜ in.
(10 mm)

2½ in.
(160 mm)

10 in.
(250 mm)

4 in.
(100 mm)

2³⁄₁₆ in.
(60 mm)

8 in.
(200 mm)

If you want to build a larger trug, go
for increased length and depth, rather
than increased width, as this would
make it rather awkward. The template
for the side upright is shown right.

**You'll need
to know**

CUTTING CURVED
SHAPES
p.18

NAILING AND
PINNING
p.24

WHITTLING
p.25

Materials

pine (see cutting list)

36 steel brads: ¾₆ in. (20 mm)

10 countersunk stainless-steel
screws: 1¼ in. (30 mm) × no. 8

sandpaper grades 80 and 100

acrylic paint: color to suit

teak oil

Cutting List

all pieces cut from pine

2 pieces 17¼ × 4 × ¾ in.
(440 × 100 × 18 mm)
(side boards)

9 pieces 10 × 1¾ × ½ in.
(250 × 45 × 12 mm) (slats)

2 pieces 8 × 2³⁄₁₆ × ¾ in.
(200 × 60 × 18 mm)
(side uprights)

1 piece 12 × 1⅝ × 1⅝ in.
(300 × 40 × 40 mm)
(stretcher handle)

FIG 1

FIG 2

1 Take the two prepared boards 17¼ in. (440
mm) long and 4 in. (100 mm) wide, and use
the bevel gauge, ruler and square to carefully
draw out the profile of the sides, complete with the
centerline and the position of the slats (see Fig 1).

2 Clamp the workpiece firmly on the bench
so that the waste is hanging over, and use
the jigsaw to cut out the profile to the waste
side of the drawn line (see Fig 2). Always cut from
the base edge through to the top corner.

FIG 3

3 Clamp the two 2³⁄₁₆ in.-(60 mm)-wide side uprights together. Use the square, ruler and compass to lay out the round-topped shape (see working drawing) complete with a centerline and the position of the handle hole (see Fig 3).

FIG 4

4 Drill the handle holes with the ⅝ in. (15 mm) forstner bit. Use the scroll saw to cut out the design, with the line of cut set slightly to the waste side of the drawn line (see Fig 4).

FIG 5

5 With the two side boards bottom edge facing up and parallel to each other, bridge them with the slats. Check the alignment with the square, and then nail the slats in position with two brads at each end (see Fig 5).

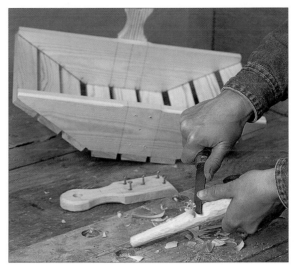

FIG 6

TIP

When you are whittling, control the knife by working with the wood braced tightly against your thumb, and making a "pushing" cut. Keep both the knife and the workpiece moving so you achieve a uniform section. Use a selection of knives of different weights and sizes, to achieve a variety of cuts.

6 Screw one side upright in place. To make the stretcher handle, whittle the 1⅝ in. (40 mm) section into a cylinder with the knife, working from center to end. Continue until the ends fit the ⅝ in. (15 mm) holes and the form is nicely curved (see Fig 6). Trap the handle between the two side uprights and fix with screws. Finally, clean up all the end-grain surfaces with the block plane and rub the trug with sandpaper. Dilute the paint in water to make a wash and brush on. When it is dry, apply two coats of teak oil.

Doll house

Most children really enjoy playing with doll houses, but many parents find them something of a nuisance. The problem is that they are usually bulky, fragile, and difficult to store. So we have designed a doll house that can be stored flat. When the children have finished playing with it, you simply pull it apart and slide it under the bed. The design is so simple that you can even let the children put it together themselves, like a construction kit. We have stylized the design so that children can let their imaginations run wild: it can be a townhouse, or a cottage, or perhaps a garage for cars, or even a school. There are many exciting possibilities.

The house is made of ¼ in. (6 mm) birch plywood, and the various forms are slotted and shaped so that the parts slide together easily. The scroll saw makes it simple to construct. Most of the corners are rounded, and the whole thing is finished with child friendly acrylic paint. Check with the manufacturer to ensure that a paint really is suitable for applying to a children's toy—it must have no harmful effects if the toy is put in the mouth.

——— Essential Tools ———

workbench with vise and holdfast, compass, pencil, ruler, square, bevel gauge, scroll saw, electric drill, ¼ in. (5 mm) and ⅜ in. (8 mm) twist bits, sanding block, 2 paintbrushes

OTHER USEFUL TOOLS
power sander

Doll house

You'll need to know

CUTTING CURVED SHAPES
p.18

SANDING
p.26

PAINTED FINISHES
p.27

The doll house is suitable for very young children to play with, as there are no tight holes where tiny fingers might get trapped.

Materials

birch plywood and pine (see cutting list)

sandpaper grades 100 and 150

acrylic paint: red, yellow, pink, blue and green

matte acrylic varnish

Cutting List

1 piece birch plywood 16 × 16 × ¼ in.
(400 × 400 × 6 mm) (bottom floor)

1 piece birch plywood 14 × 14 × ¼ in.
(350 × 350 × 6 mm) (middle floor)

2 pieces birch plywood 12 × 6⅝ × ¼ in.
(300 × 170 × 6 mm) (roof flaps)

1 piece birch plywood 16 × 14 × ¼ in.
(400 × 350 × 6 mm) (ridge wall)

1 piece birch plywood 16 × 14 × ¼ in.
(400 × 350 × 6 mm) (gable wall)

4 pieces birch plywood 5⅝ × 5³⁄₁₆ × ¼ in.
(140 × 130 × 6 mm) (stairs)

2 × 1⅝ in. (40 mm) lengths of ⁵⁄₁₆ in. (8 mm) pine dowel

FIG 1

1 Study the working drawings carefully to see how the whole thing works and slots together, and then use the rule, bevel gauge, and square to lay out each piece of plywood with all the lines that make up the design (see Fig 1). Shade in the waste areas up to the drawn line.

FIG 3

3 When you come to an enclosed area—such as the doors or the roof slots—drill pilot holes with the ¼ in. (5 mm) bit. Unhitch the scroll saw blade, pass it through the hole, and then refit it and continue as already described (see Fig 3). Be careful not to twist the blade at the turns.

FIG 2

2 Fit a new fine blade in the scroll saw and tension it until it "pings" when plucked, then start cutting out the various parts (see Fig 2). When you are cutting the slots, make sure that you keep on the waste side of the drawn lines, so the slots are exactly ¼ in. (6 mm) wide or to a maximum of ½₂ in. (0.5 mm) wider, making ⅗₂ in. (6.5 mm).

FIG 4

4 Run through a trial fitting of the two walls (see Fig 4). If the slots are too tight, wrap a sheet of fine-grade sandpaper around a piece of waste plywood and sand them to fit. Aim to increase the width of the slots to a maximum of ⅗₂ in. (6.5 mm). Be careful not to rub so hard that you expose the inner veneers of the plywood.

FIG 5

5 Slide the bottom floor over the walls and check that it fits well—it should sit flat on all four of the lower support steps. Slide the middle floor in place so that it settles on all four of the upper support steps (see Fig 5). Once again, you might need to adjust the slots with fine-grade sandpaper. The best way of sanding is to rest the workpiece flat on the bench, so that the offending edge is as near as possible to the worksurface.

FIG 6

6 Take one of the stair pieces and draw on a ⅜ in. (10 mm) grid, the outline of the stairs, arched door and dowel holes. Stack the four stair pieces with the gridded piece on top, then drill holes with the ⁵⁄₁₆ in. (8 mm) bit and slide in the dowels. With the scroll saw, cut the shapes of the stairs and door through the whole stack (see Fig 6).

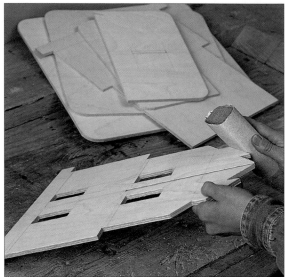

FIG 7

7 Take the sanding block and sandpaper and rub all the edges to a good, smooth finish (see Fig 7). Aim for slightly rounded edges. A good way of testing for burrs or sharp edges that you have missed is to feel the forms with your fingertips, keeping your eyes closed.

TIP

Of all the projects in this book, this is the only one where you cannot cut costs—children's toys must be safe. You must use best-quality birch plywood, because it is strong and splinter-proof. It is essential to use paints (and varnishes) that are described by the manufacturer as being safe for children: on no account use household or car paints, because they may contain toxic substances.

FIG 8

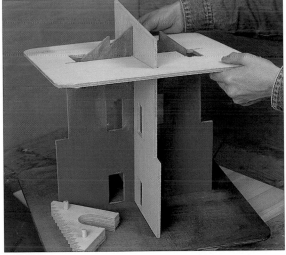

FIG 9

8 Mix the paint with a small amount of water to make a thin wash, apply with a brush (see Fig 8) and let it dry. If you want the color to be darker, you simply paint on repeat washes until you have the right density of color. Let the washes dry between coats.

9 When the paint is completely dry—and this might take a couple of days—give the house another sanding with the graded sandpaper and brush on the varnish. Repeat this procedure a couple of times until the finish feels very smooth to the touch (see Fig 9).

Construction variations

Alternative construction idea to make an open-fronted room (shown below)

Staircase made from shaped blocks glued to a plywood backing

Hinged roof locates over the chimney stack

Doors cut into the middle of the house creating a view through into all the top rooms

Child's folk art chest

When our two sons were about five years old, we made them a traditional six-board chest. It was only a box painted blue, with rope handles and an old map pasted on the underside of the lid, but they thought that it was wonderful. In their imaginations it became a treasure chest and numerous other exciting things. When they were older, it was used to store clothes.

The chest is made from pine throughout. The front and back boards are screwed to the end boards, with the baseboard trapped and screwed in between. Rope handles are threaded and knotted through blocks. The lid is simply set flush with the back and hinged. The painted design is in the style of the naïve designs on old American folk art chests. Although we have used red, white, and blue, and stars and stripes, we have not painted the chest with the specific imagery of the American or British flags. The stripes are painted with the aid of masking tape; the stars are created by cutting a star from a scrap of plywood and using it as a stamp.

Essential Tools

workbench with vise, compass, pencil, ruler, square, scroll saw, electric drill, ¼ in. (6 mm) counterbore bit with a plug cutter to match, screwdriver bit, block plane, clamps, benchtop drill press, ⅜ in. (10 mm) and ¼ in. (5 mm) twist bits, countersink bit, sanding block, scissors, ¾ in. (20 mm) bevel-edge chisel, artist's paintbrush, screwdriver, paintbrush

OTHER USEFUL TOOLS
power sander

Child's folk art chest

24 in. (600 mm)

17 in. (425 mm)

1¼ in. (30 mm) radius

6 in. (150 mm)

4 in. (100 mm)

1 in. (25 mm)

14 in. (350 mm)

18 in. (450 mm)

19⅝ in. (490 mm)

2¾ in. (70 mm)

2 in. (50 mm) radius

14 in. (350 mm)

4 in. (100 mm)

1⅜ in. (35 mm) diameter

Star stamp

6 in. (150 mm)

1¼ in. (30 mm)

1 in. (26 mm)

1⅜ in. (35 mm)

1 in. (25 mm)

1⅝ in. (40 mm)

Handle block

You'll need to know

CUTTING CURVED SHAPES
p.18

PAINTED FINISHES
p.27

ATTACHING HINGES
p.25

Materials

pine (see cutting list)

30 countersunk steel screws:
1¼ in. (30 mm) × no. 8

PVA glue

sandpaper grades 100 and 150

6 countersunk steel screws:
1½ in. (35 mm) × no. 8

2 × 12 in. (300 mm) lengths of soft hemp rope

masking tape and scissors

acrylic paint: red, white and blue

2 steel hinges: 2 × ¾ in. (50 × 18 mm) with screws to fit

Danish oil

When you are attaching the rope handles, make sure that you make the loops much smaller than the size of your child's head, or the handles will present a safety hazard.

Cutting List

all pieces cut from pine

2 pieces 19⅝ × 14 × ¾ in.
(490 × 350 × 18 mm) (front and back boards)

2 pieces 18 × 14 × ¾ in.
(450 × 350 × 18 mm) (end boards)

1 piece 18⅛ × 14 × ¾ in.
(454 × 350 × 18 mm) (baseboard)

1 piece 24 × 17 × ¾ in.
(600 × 425 × 18 mm) (lid board)

2 pieces 6 × 1⅝ × 1 in.
(150 × 40 × 25 mm) (handle blocks)

FIG 1

1 Check all the wood to make sure that it is free from splits. Take the prepared boards and use the ruler, square, and compass to draw out all the lines that make up the design. Lay out the curve of the lid corners with a 1¼ in. (30 mm) radius, and the foot detail on the end boards with a radius of 2 in. (50 mm) (see Fig 1). Double-check the measurements and shade in selected areas to avoid confusion when cutting out. Draw the shape of the handle blocks, complete with holes.

FIG 2

2 Cut out the various shapes on the scroll saw. When you are cutting the curves, run the line of cut to the waste side of the drawn line (see Fig 2). Have a trial fitting to see how the box goes together. Pay particular attention to the fit of the baseboard.

FIG 4

4 Trim the baseboard to fit between the sides of the chest and fix with 1¼ in. (30 mm) screws, using the drill and screwdriver attachment, as described in step 3 (see Fig 4). Turn the chest upright to see whether it stands firm. If it rocks, the feet need trimming with the block plane.

FIG 3

3 With the ¼ in. (6 mm) counterbore bit, drill pilot holes through the front and back boards. Using the drill and screwdriver attachment, screw them to the end boards with the 1¼ in. (30 mm) screws (see Fig 3). The top edges should be flush. Check all angles with the square. Cut plugs with the plug cutter and glue them over the screws.

FIG 5

5 Cut the handle blocks with the scroll saw and draw in the position of the holes: two ⅜ in. (10 mm) holes for the ropes, and three ³⁄₁₆ in. (5 mm) holes for the screws. Clamp to the benchtop drill press and bore the holes (see Fig 5). Countersink the screwholes with the countersink bit and sand the blocks to a smooth finish.

FIG 6

6 Measure 4 in. (100 mm) down from the top of the chest, and center and screw the handle blocks in place with 1½ in. (35 mm) screws (see Fig 6). Take a 12 in. (300 mm) length of rope, thread it through the holes and knot the ends. Tie figure eight knots so they cannot slip and come undone.

FIG 7

7 To make the stamp, set the compass to a radius of 1½ in. (35 mm) and draw a circle on scrap wood. With the compass at the same radius, make step-offs around the circumference of the circle and draw arcs. Use the pencil and ruler to draw lines between alternate intersections, so you end up with a six-pointed star (see Fig 7).

FIG 8

8 Position the chest with the front facing up. Measure 2 in. (50 mm) in from all four edges and use the pencil and ruler to draw a border or frame. Divide up the inside area vertically, so that you have four equal horizontal bands each about 2⅛ in. (60 mm) wide. From top to bottom number the bands 1, 2, 3, and 4. Cover the outer frame and bands 2 and 4 with masking tape. Smooth the tape in place. Brush red acrylic paint over bands 1 and 3, painting well over the edges of the tape. Leave it to dry (see Fig 8).

FIG 9

9 When the red paint is dry, carefully peel off the horizontal strips of tape to reveal beautiful, crisp edges (see Fig 9). Stick masking tape over the bands of red to safeguard them.

FIG 10

FIG 11

11 Cut out the star on the scroll saw, sand the edges to a smooth finish, and drive a 1¼ in. (30 mm) screw into its center to use like a handle. Spread a generous amount of white paint on a piece of cardboard, then press the star in the paint and start stamping (see Fig 11). Try to do the stamping with a neat on-and-off action, so the images do not smudge.

10 Paint the bands that you have just revealed with blue paint (see Fig 10). Let the paint dry and carefully peel away all the masking tape on the bands and borders. You should be left with a neatly painted panel. At this point, if you wish, you could paint similar bands on the lid of the chest.

TIP

If you like the idea of a printed design, but do not want to use the stars, you could cut an alternative shape, or try using other items as stamps, such as corks or leaves. Use paint straight from the tube or bottle, so that it is a thick consistency and will not run.

FIG 12

12 Finally, when the paint is dry, use the chisel to cut recesses for the hinges and screw them in place. Sand all the surfaces with fine-grade sandpaper, followed by a coat of Danish oil (see Fig 12).

Kitchen cart

Now at last you can have the custom made kitchen cart of your dreams! A modern classic, this beautifully designed kitchen workstation is made from cool, blonde maple. The woven basket drawer is English willow, the towel bar is stainless steel, the worktop is made from chunky sections, and the cart is mounted on four super-smooth, swivel-turn wheels. This is an amazingly stylish and functional piece—perfect for the modern home.

As for the making process, study our designs first, purchase a ready-made willow basket, the wheels and stainless steel fittings, and then modify the dimensions and details to suit your needs. It's an easy project to build. The horizontal members—the front and back stretchers, and the back rail— are tenoned into the legs to make two H-frames, and then the two frames are linked by the side rails, the top board, and the shelf slats. The wheels are bolted into pilot holes, while the top slab is held in place with screwed blocks and turnbuckles. The wood is finished by repeatedly rubbing, oiling, waxing, and burnishing to a sheen finish with a cotton cloth.

Essential Tools

workbench with vise, pencil, ruler, square, biscuit joiner, 4 sash clamps or clamp heads, good selection of C-clamps, jigsaw, block plane, scraper plane, benchtop drill press, 1 in. (25 mm) forstner bit, ⅛ in. (3 mm) and ³⁄₁₆ in. (5 mm) twist bits and a twist bit to fit the diameter of your wheel bolts, ⅝ in. (15 mm) bevel-edge chisel, mallet, miter saw, router and router table, ½ in. (12 mm) groove cutter, knife, tenon saw, smoothing plane, screwdriver, sanding block, countersink bit, socket and wrench to fit the size of your wheel bolt, paintbrush

OTHER USEFUL TOOLS
cordless screwdriver, power sander, electric drill, dividers, marking knife, bandsaw

Kitchen cart

25 in.
(630 mm)

25 in.
(630 mm)

9 in.
(225 mm)

21³⁄₁₆ in.
(530 mm)

28³⁄₈ in.
(710 mm)

22 in.
(550 mm)

3¾ in.
(95 mm)

4 in.
(100 mm)

You'll need to know

HAND CUTTING A MORTISE
p.20

HAND CUTTING A TENON
p.21

ROUTING A MORTISE
p.21

Materials

maple (see cutting list)

pack of joiner biscuits

PVA glue

sandpaper grades 150 to 300

4 swivel-turn wheels (with foot brakes), to stand about 4 in. (100 mm) from the floor

Danish oil

28 countersunk stainless-steel screws: 1¼ in. (30 mm) × no. 8

stainless-steel towel rack

Cutting List

all pieces cut from maple

5 pieces 25 × 5⅝ × 1³⁄₁₆ in.
(630 × 140 × 30 mm) (worktop)

4 pieces 28³⁄₈ × 2 × 2 in.
(710 × 50 × 50 mm) (legs)

2 pieces 21³⁄₁₆ × 3³⁄₁₆ × ¾ in.
(530 × 80 × 20 mm) (side rails)

1 piece 20⅛ × 3³⁄₁₆ × ¾ in.
(510 × 80 × 20 mm) (back rail)

4 pieces 22 × 1³⁄₁₆ × 1³⁄₁₆ in.
(550 × 30 × 30 mm) (stretchers)

10 pieces 23⅝ × 2¾ × 2¾ in.
(590 × 70 × 12) mm (shelf slats)

If your wheels are a different size than those specified, be sure to adjust the length of the legs accordingly.

FIG 1

1 Take the five prepared boards for the worktop [25 in. (630 mm) long, 5⅝ in. (140 mm) wide)], and place them side by side so that the end grain in neighboring boards runs in different directions.

Mark in the position of the biscuit joints at the center and 2 in. (50 mm) from the ends. Set the biscuit joiner to ⅝ in. (15 mm) and cut the slots on the five boards. Blow out the dust and spread glue on the mating faces of the biscuits and the boards, and clamp them. Use three sash clamps, plus the C-clamps, to hold the joints in place (see Fig 1).

When the glue is completely dry, remove the clamps and move the slab to a clean, level surface. Finally, use the jigsaw, block plane, and scraper plane to work the slab to a smooth, clean-edged finish, 25 in. (630 mm) square. Remove all traces of glue.

FIG 2

2 Take the four 28⅜ in. (710 mm) legs and mark the top and bottom. Set out mortises 1 in. (25 mm) square, at centers 9 in. (225 mm) down from the top and 3¾ in. (95 mm) up from the bottom. Draw crossed diagonals to establish the position of the wheel bolts. Drill the mortises with the 1 in. (25 mm) forstner bit, to a depth of 1½ in. (40 mm). Drill holes in the ends of the legs to fit your wheel bolts (see Fig 2).

FIG 4

4 Take the four 22 in. (550 mm) stretchers and lay out the tenons by measuring 1½ in. (40 mm) from the ends. Set the miter saw depth gauge to ⅛ in. (2.5 mm) and saw the tenon shoulders (see Fig 4). Use the chisel to pare the tenons to fit. Aim for a tight push-fit, with the shoulders of the tenon sitting square and flush with the face of the leg. Test that it is square with the square.

FIG 3

3 Clamp the legs to the bench and use the bevel edge chisel and the mallet to work the bored holes into crisp, blind mortises 1 in. (25 mm) square and 1½ in. (40 mm) deep (see Fig 3). Scrape the bottom of the mortise to a clean finish and remove all the debris. Be careful not to lever the tool against the side of the mortise.

FIG 5

5 Mark out open rail mortises on the legs, at 3 in. (75 mm) long, ½ in. (12 mm) wide and ¾ in. (20 mm) deep, and centered so that the rails are set ⅜ in. (10 mm) back from the face. Attach the router to its table, fit the ½ in. (12 mm) groove cutter, set the fence to %6 in. (14 mm), clamp a stop block made from a piece of scrap at 3 in. (75 mm), and rout the mortises (see Fig 5).

FIG 6

6 Mark the ends of the rails at ¾ in. (20 mm). Rout the stepped tenons, making them ¾ in. (20 mm) long, 3 in. (75 mm) wide and ½ in. (12 mm) thick. Use the knife to whittle the stepped underside so that it fits into the ½ in. (12 mm) open mortise (see Fig 6).

FIG 7

7 Plane the worktop to a square finish with the smoothing plane. Use the biscuit joiner to cut grooves on the inside face of both side rails. Use the tenon saw to cut turnbuckles and screw blocks (see Fig 7) from scrap wood to fit.

Clear the workbench of accumulated clutter and use a vacuum cleaner to remove all small pieces of debris. If the top of your workbench is badly scarred or covered in hard blobs of glue, cover it with a sheet of clean plywood to work on. It is vital that the surface is perfectly clean. Set the worktop face down on the workbench or ply-

wood, and make a dry run fitting of the legs, stretchers, and rails (see Fig 7).

When you are happy with the way it all goes together, spread glue in the joints and clamp them. When the glue is dry, remove the clamps, screw the blocks and the turnbuckles in place to hold the worktop to the rails, and use the chisel and the sandpaper to remove all traces of dried glue.

> ## TIP
>
> To avoid drill chatter and friction burns when countersinking the holes, fix the drill's depth gauge to ³⁄₁₆ in. (5 mm) and then swiftly and firmly run the countersink bit in and out. Make sure the drill is running at full speed before the bit strikes the wood.

FIG 8

8 Take two of the shelf slats and mark the position of the screwholes 1 in. (25 mm) from the ends—one with a single hole at the center and the other with two holes ¾ in. (20 mm) in from the sides. Double-check your measurements.

Use the two slats to build a jig from scrap wood, and then drill all the slats with the ³⁄₁₆ in. (5 mm) twist bit and the countersink bit (see Fig 8).

Make sure, after every drilling, that you stop and use a brush to remove the sawdust from the corners of the jig. Work carefully so that the drill bit enters and exits leaving clean holes.

FIG 9

FIG 10

9 Clear all the dust and fragments of wood off the workbench and set the trolley upside-down on the bench, so that the ends of the legs are at a comfortable height. With the socket and wrench, bolt the wheels in place (see Fig 9). Go over the trolley with the block plane, cleaning up ends and trimming sharp corners. Make sure that all traces of glue have been removed. To this end, take the trolley outside the workshop, so that you can view it in full daylight, and inspect all the areas around the joints. A good test is to brush the surface with mineral spirits, which will highlight any areas of glue. Finally, sweep up the debris and wipe the dust off with a cotton cloth.

10 Move to a clean area and brush the whole trolley with a thin coat of Danish oil, working over the frame with the worktop in place and the ten loose slats.

Set the two hole slats to bridge the stretchers, so that they are up against the legs with the ends flush (see Fig 10). Drill ⅛ in. (3 mm) pilot holes and attach the slats in place with the stainless-steel screws. Lay out the single hole slats with a spacing of 1¼ in. (30 mm) and repeat the screwing procedure. To ensure that the spacing is uniform, cut a strip of waste 1¼ in. (30 mm) wide, and set it between neighboring slats before driving the screws in. Screw the stainless-steel rail in place.

Construction variations

Stretcher dowel joined to leg instead of mortise and tenon

Stretcher screwed to leg

Stretcher lap-joined and screwed to leg

Protective stainless-steel end to leg

Worktop made from square sections of wood, with the end grain showing on the surface

French cupboard

This pretty little herb cupboard was inspired by a cupboard that we saw about twenty years ago when on a walking vacation in southern France. We looked though a farmhouse window and there it was, perfectly captured in a shaft of sunlight. It was a very simple construction, really not much more than a fruit crate—perhaps it was even made from scrap wood.

Our design is lifted above the ordinary by beautifully delicate curves at top and bottom, a colorwashed finish, and a whittled handle that doubles as a catch. The cupboard is made from good quality pine tongue and groove boards for the front, back, sides, and shelves; pine sections for the door battens and shelf supports inside, to hold the whole thing together; and a piece of scrap for the handle. The surface is colorwashed with a mixture of acrylic paint and water, and finally wiped over with teak oil. We chose a mix of blue and green to achieve a greenish tinge, but you can opt for any color that appeals, such as a strong red, or even a whitewashed finish.

Essential Tools

workbench with vise, pencil, ruler, square, smoothing plane, screwdriver, scroll saw, sanding block, miter saw, ¼ in. (7 mm) counterbore bit with a plug cutter to match, knife, electric drill, ⅜ in. (10 mm) and ⅛ in. (3 mm) twist bits, awl, 2 paintbrushes

OTHER USEFUL TOOLS
cordless screwdriver, power sander, marking knife

French cupboard

You'll need to know

SCREWING
p.24

CUTTING CURVED SHAPES
p.18

WHITTLING
p.25

8 in. (200 mm)

13½ in. (338 mm)

5⅝ in. (140 mm)

4 in. (100 mm)

26 in. (650 mm)

28 in. (700 mm)

4 in. (100 mm)

4 in. (100 mm)

3¼ in. (80 mm) 3½ in. (89 mm) 3½ in. (89 mm) 3¼ in. (80 mm)

Materials

pine (see cutting list)

50+ countersunk steel screws:
1½ in. (35 mm) × no. 8

sandpaper grades 80 and 150

2 surface-mounted brass hinges
(design and size to suit) with screws to fit

acrylic paint: color to suit

teak oil

Cutting List

all pieces cut from pine

4 pieces of tongue-and-groove
28 × 3½ × ⅝ in.
(700 × 89 × 15 mm) (front boards,
consisting of 2 doors and 2 side pieces)

4 pieces of tongue-and-groove
26 × 3½ × ⅝ in.
(650 × 89 × 15 mm) (back boards)

4 pieces of tongue-and-groove
26 × 3½ × ⅝ in.
(650 × 89 × 15 mm((side boards)

3 pieces 12½ × 6¾ × ¾ in.
(312 × 170 × 18 mm) (shelves)

8 pieces 6³⁄₁₆ × 1¼ × ¾ in.
(160 × 30 × 18 mm)
(2 door battens and 6 shelf supports)

If you want to carve a more complex catch than this one (which is made of leftover scraps), consider using a piece of easy-to-carve basswood.

FIG 1

FIG 2

1 Study the design and note how all the boards that meet at the corners have been reduced in width. Now take the smoothing plane and trim the boards to size (see Fig 1).

2 Take the two boards that make the door and screw them together with two 6³⁄₁₆ in. (160 mm) door battens. Use two staggered screws on each board width (see Fig 2).

FIG 3

3 Set the four front boards together (the two doors at center and a side piece on either side), flex the ruler across the top and draw the curved profile (see Fig 2). Get help if needed. Repeat this procedure for the other end.

FIG 5

5 Take the six 6⅜₆ in. (160 mm) shelf supports (two to support each shelf, two to support the top of the cupboard and two to support the bottom) and use the miter saw to cut one end of each piece to 45° (see Fig 5).

FIG 4

4 Take the door (all screwed together) and with the curved ends clearly marked, very carefully cut the curved profile on the scroll saw (see Fig 4). Cut the two side boards in the same way. Sand the sawed edges to a smooth, slightly rounded, and blurred finish.

FIG 6

6 Take the three 12½ in. (312 mm) shelf boards and screw the 6⅜₆ in. (160 mm) shelf supports to the ends, so that the square end of the support is flush with the back edge of the shelf board (see Fig 6). Use the block and sandpaper to rub all edges and ends to a smooth finish.

FIG 7

FIG 9

7 Screw the three shelf boards to the paired side boards (see Fig 7). Note that the middle shelf is placed so that the supports are on the underside, with the mitered ends facing what will be the front of the cupboard. Screw the other two side boards in place.

9 Whittle the three components that make the door catch—the piece that screws to the side of the cupboard, the latch and the central swivel. There is no need to copy our design exactly, just study it to see how it functions and then go for a similar form. Drill through the latch with the ⅜ in. (10 mm) bit and slide the central swivel in place. Drill a ⅛ in. (3 mm) hole through the side of the unit and fix with a dowel whittled from a scrap [make it 4 in. (100) mm long and ⅛ in. (3 mm) in diameter]. Continue carving the catch components until the form is to your liking (see Fig 9). Use a fold of sandpaper wrapped around a stick to sculpt the wood to a smooth shape and finish.

FIG 8

8 Screw the four backboards in place, with screws running through into the edges of the shelves and the side boards (see Fig 8). The screws should be flush with the surface. Screw the front of the cupboard in place, this time sinking the holes with the counterbore bit so that the screws will lie well below the surface.

FIG 10

10

Set the door in place, mark the screw-holes with the awl and screw the hinges in place. Depending upon the size of your chosen hinges, position one about 5⅝ in. (140 mm) down from the top and the other about 4 in. (100 mm) up from the bottom (see Fig 10). Use a fold of fine-grade sandpaper to roughen the surface of the brass hinges and dull the shine.

FIG 11

11

Screw the catch to the side of the cupboard and use it to establish the position of the swivel latch. Mark the pivot point with a pencil, and drill with the ⅜ in. (10 mm) bit. Slide the central peg in place (see Fig 11). Drill a hole in the peg with the ⅛ in. (3 mm) bit, on the inside face of the door. Whittle a pin with the knife and slide it through to hold the latch in place.

Sand all the surfaces with the graded sandpapers. Dilute the paint in water and colorwash the cupboard. When it is dry, sand all the surfaces to a smooth finish—cutting through the paint to reveal the grain—and wipe all the surfaces with teak oil. With the plug cutter, cut little plugs from scrap wood and glue them in the counterbored holes to cover the screwheads.

TIP

It's a good idea to experiment with colorwashing before you tackle the cupboard. Thin some acrylic paint with water and paint a piece of scrap wood, then sand and oil as described. If you want the color to be lighter or darker, you simply add more water or paint accordingly. Remember that sawn edges and light grain absorb more color and look darker.

Construction variations

Barefaced housing joint

H-shaped hinges

Doors are rabbeted where they meet at the center

Beaded detail for tongue-and-groove panelling

Door construction with chamfered edges on the cross pieces

T-shaped hinges

Adjustable porch chair

If you would like to build a quick and easy porch chair, this classic "crate" design is sure to please. The project draws its inspiration from the work of Gerrit Rietveld (1888–1957), the Dutch designer and architect, and member of the De Stijl group, who developed designs that could be made from salvaged wood. It's a stylish chair, perfect for the porch, conservatory, or studio. The back can be adjusted. If you want to relax and stretch out for a doze, you simply withdraw the two gate bolts in order to lower the back.

The chair is made from American oak, and the boards are joined with screws and toggle fasteners. The great thing about the design is that the whole chair can be made without having to cut any joints. The boards are simply butted or sandwiched and then fitted with toggle fasteners running through the thickness. The two H-frames that make up the arms are linked by the seat frame in such a way that the back can be fixed in either an upright or horizontal mode. To finish the surface of the wood, it is vigorously wire-brushed to give it a weathered texture and wiped with Danish oil.

Essential Tools

workbench with vise, compass, pencil, ruler, square, C-clamps, benchtop drill press, ⅜ in. (10 mm) and ⅝ in. (15 mm) forstner bits, ³⁄₁₆ in. (5 mm) twist bit, scroll saw, 2 sash clamps, block plane, sanding block, wire brush, paintbrush, countersink bit, screwdriver, hacksaw, metal file, allen key to fit the hex-heads

OTHER USEFUL TOOLS
cordless screwdriver, power sander, electric drill, dividers, marking knife

Adjustable porch chair

You'll need to know

DRILLING HOLES
p.19

CUTTING CURVED SHAPES
p.18

SPECIAL FINISHES
p.27

3 in. (72.5 mm) radius

5¾ in. (145 mm) radius

5¾ in. (145 mm)

5¾ in. (145 mm)

5¾ in. (145 mm)

This design allows the back to be positioned up or down, but you could easily add more holes in order to have a choice of back positions.

chair back is pivoted on a toggle fastener

arm is made from 2 pieces of wood

5¾ in. (145 mm) radius

24 in. (600 mm)

18 in. (450 mm)

5¾ in. (145 mm) radius

18 in. (450 mm)

18 in. (450 mm)

1³⁄₁₆ in. (27.5 mm)

19⅝ in. (490 mm)

Materials

American oak (see cutting list)

PVA glue

sandpaper grades 100 and 150

mineral spirits

cloth

Danish oil

35 countersunk steel screws: 1¼ in. (30 mm) × no. 8

16 steel and brass hex-head toggle fasteners complete with threaded steel rod to fit

2 steel gate bolts with screws: to fit a ⅜ in. (10 mm) hole

Cutting List

all pieces cut from American oak

4 pieces 18 × 5¾ × ¾ in.
(450 × 145 × 20 mm) (leg boards)

2 pieces 24 × 5¾ × ¾ in.
(600 × 145 × 20 mm) (horizontal side boards)

3 pieces 18 × 5¾ × ¾ in.
(450 × 145 × 20 mm) (seat boards)

2 pieces 19⅝ × 2³⁄₁₆ × ¾ in.
(490 × 55 × 20 mm) (seat battens)

3 pieces 27 × 5¾ × ¾ in.
(675 × 145 × 20 mm) (backboards)

2 pieces 17¾ × 5¾ × ¾ in.
(445 × 145 × 20 mm) (back battens)

2 pieces 24 × 2³⁄₁₆ × ¾ in.
(600 × 55 × 20 mm) (arm battens)

2 pieces 18 × 5¾ × ¾ in.
(450 × 145 × 20 mm) (arm boards)

1 piece 21⅜ × 5¾ × ¾ in.
(540 × 145 × 20 mm) (back frame board)

FIG 1

1 Study the working drawing and work out the position of the various drilled holes. Build a simple jig using workshop scraps, and clamp the jig to the benchtop drill press with C-clamps. Set to work drilling the blind holes to fit the brass hex-heads, using the ⅝ in. (15 mm) forstner bit (see Fig 1). Drill to a depth of ³⁄₁₆ in. (5 mm).

FIG 2

2 Change to the ⅜ in. (10 mm) forstner bit and continue the hole through the thickness of the wood (see Fig 2). Repeat this procedure for all the hex-head holes. Use the ⅜ in. (10 mm) forstner bit for the toggle holes, and the ³⁄₁₆ in. (5 mm) twist bit for the screw and rod holes.

FIG 3

3 Take the three 27 in. (675 mm) back boards, decide on the best ends and faces, and use the compass to lay out the top details. Use a radius of 3 in. (72.5 mm) for the middle board, and 5¾ in. (145 mm) for the other two (see Fig 3). If you can get an adjustable compass, it is better because the legs stay put and will not slip.

FIG 4

4 Fit a new fine-toothed blade in the scroll saw, make adjustments to ensure maximum tension, and then cut out the top ends of the three back boards (see Fig 4). If you work at a slow pace, the sawn edge will turn out to be so smooth that it will hardly need sanding.

FIG 5

5 Take one of the 18 in. (450 mm) arm boards, set the compass to a radius of 5¾ in. (145 mm) and scribe the back end of the board with the quarter-circle curve that makes the design. Cut out the curve on the scroll saw and keep the piece of quarter-circle waste for the arm bracket. Take the cut arm board and one of the 24 in. (600 mm) arm battens, spread glue on mating side faces and clamp them together with the sash clamps (see Fig 5). Be careful not to overtighten the clamps so that they buckle. When the glue is dry, scribe an identical quarter-circle curve on the front end of the arm and fret it out on the scroll saw. Repeat this procedure for the other arm.

FIG 6

6 Use the block plane and sandpaper to work the end-grain surfaces of all components to a good finish, chamfering all the corners and edges. Wire-brush all surfaces. Remove the dust with a cloth dampened in mineral spirits and brush all the surfaces with Danish oil (see Fig 6).

FIG 7

7 To build the seat, set the two 19⅜ in. (490 mm) seat battens flat on the bench and bridge them with the three 18 in. (450 mm) seat boards. Use a piece of wood ³⁄₁₆ in. (27.5 mm) thick to space the boards precisely the same distance apart. Check battens with the square and ruler, drill screwholes with the countersink bit, and attach the boards in place with screws (see Fig 7).

TIP

Depending upon the manufacturer, hex-head toggle fasteners come in many shapes, types, and sizes. They may be made of stainless steel or plastic rather than brass, and the hex-head size may differ. So you might need to use a different sized drill bit to suit the particular design and size of your fitting. Buy the fittings and experiment on scrap wood to ascertain the necessary drill size.

FIG 8

FIG 9

9 Screw the arm bracket to the inside edge of the front leg board and fit the arm board with the toggle fasteners (see Fig 9). Repeat on the other arm. Check with the square.

8 To build the side H-frames, take two 18 in. (450 mm) vertical leg boards and bridge them with the 24 in. (600 mm) horizontal side board (with one leg under and the other over). Slide the toggle fasteners in place (hex-heads, toggle and threaded rod cut to length with the hacksaw and cleaned up with the file), and use the allen key to tighten up just enough to grip. Check with the square, and complete necessary adjustments to the alignment. Tighten the toggle fasteners to make the whole thing stable (see Fig 8). Repeat this procedure for the other H-frame. While the two H-frames are identical in every respect, they are also mirror image copies of each other, as are the arms of most chairs.

FIG 10

10 Finally, when you have pivoted the seat back on the toggle fasteners—as shown in the working drawing—and screwed the horizontal backboard in place, attach the two gate bolts (see Fig 10).

Construction variations

Peg and a choice of holes allow for back adjustment

Space for magazines

Rounded end on the armrest

A series of notches allow for adjustment

Side view of one of the notches shown above

Large hole for washer and nut

Bolted butt joint

Log holder

This design is a coming together of many shapes that we have seen over the years. It looks a little like a dough holder once spotted in a baker's shop in Leicestershire, the handle owes its shape to a New England knife tray in the American Museum in Bath, but most of all, this holder draws its inspiration from an early nineteenth-century washing holder that we found in our house in Cornwall. All these holders have certain things in common: a characteristic canted boat-like shape, the way the pierced handle strip is fixed to the end board, and the color green. The appealing thing about them is the fact that while the woodworker needed to do no more than make a functional box—for washing clothes, baking and such—he found time to make it into a decorative form.

This log holder is made from pine and plywood. The shaped handle strip is screwed to the end board, while the sides are nailed to the ends. It's a surprisingly challenging project. If you are interested in building other holders and need inspiration, visit a rural life museum to see the beautiful holders used in the house, dairy, and garden.

─────────── Essential Tools ───────────

workbench with vise and holdfast, compass, pencils,
ruler, square, bevel gauge, benchtop drill press,
³⁄₁₆ in. (5 mm) and ⁵⁄₁₆ in. (8 mm) twist bits, scroll saw,
2 short sash clamps, screwdriver, spokeshave, block
plane, router and router table, ⅜ in. (10 mm) groove
cutter, sanding block, medium hammer, paintbrush

OTHER USEFUL TOOLS
cordless screwdriver, power sander, electric drill,
dividers, marking knife

Log holder

12 in. (300 mm)

20 in. (500 mm)

3³⁄₁₆ in. (80 mm)

4⅜ in. (110 mm)

4⅜ in. (110 mm)

⅜ in. (10 mm) gap

¾ in. (20 mm) radius

groove 1 in. (25 mm) up from the bottom edge

8 in. (200 mm)

4 in. (100 mm)

10 in. (250 mm)

4 in. (100 mm)

5 in. (125 mm)

2 in. (48 mm)

Because of the difficulties of cutting and angling the side, the plywood baseboard is best cut to fit after you have had a trial fitting.

Materials

pine and plywood (see cutting list)

tracing paper 12 × 3³⁄₁₆ in. (300 × 80 mm)

PVA glue

4 countersunk steel screws: 2³⁄₁₆ in. (60 mm) × no. 8

sandpaper grades 80 to 100

24 × 2 in. (50 mm) galvanized nails

matte oil based or acrylic paint: green

mineral spirits to clean brush

Cutting List

4 pieces pine 20 × 4⅜ × ¾ in.
(500 × 110 × 18 mm) (side boards)

2 pieces pine 12 × 8¾ × ¾ in.
(300 × 220 × 18 mm) (end boards)

2 pieces pine 12 × 3³⁄₁₆ × ¾ in.
(300 × 80 × 18 mm) (handle strips)

1 piece plywood 16 × 12 × ¼ in.
(400 × 300 × 6 mm) (baseboard)

FIG 1

1 Take your piece of tracing paper—the same size as the handle strip—and fold it in half along its length so that the crease becomes the centerline. Use a soft pencil to carefully draw one half of the shape of the handle on the tracing paper. Establish the centerlines on the two handle strips. Pressing with a hard pencil, transfer the shape of the handle through to both pieces of wood. Shade in the waste so that there is no doubting what needs to be cut away (see Fig 1). You might need to adjust the handle to fit your hand.

FIG 2

FIG 4

2 Take the four side boards and use the bevel gauge, ruler, and square to draw the overall shape of the angled side. Use the ruler and compass to draw the foot detail on the two bottom side boards (see Fig 2).

4 Cut out the shape of the side boards on the scroll saw (see Fig 4). Work at a steady pace, cutting to the waste side of the drawn line. Next, cut out the shape of the two end boards. Label all the component parts with a pencil.

FIG 3

FIG 5

3 Take the handle strips and drill the screwholes. Drill the ³⁄₁₆ in. (5 mm) pilot holes completely through the wood, then re-drill the hole with a ⁵⁄₁₆ in. (8 mm) bit to a depth of ³⁄₁₆ in. (30 mm) (so the screw can be sunk). Cut out the shape of the handle on the scroll saw. When you cut the handle hole, enter and exit the blade where the pointed detail meets the edge (see Fig 3).

5 Take one end board and a cut out handle strip, spread glue on mating edges and clamp them. Drive the screws into the pilot holes and then remove the two clamps (see Fig 5). Repeat this procedure for the other end.

FIG 6

7 Use the block plane, set to a fine cut, to swiftly chamfer all sides and ends of the side boards (see Fig 7). Don't aim for a really exquisite finish—small irregularities are in keeping with the style of the project.

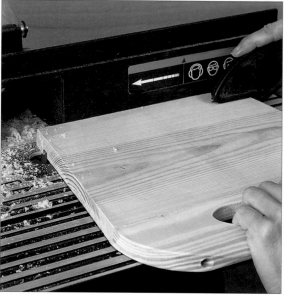

FIG 8

6 When the glue is dry, set the end board in the vice. Use the spokeshave to plane the top edge of the end board to a slightly rounded, smooth finish (see Fig 6). Work from center to side so you do not split the wood by running the blade into the end grain.

Take a fold of sandpaper and rub the inside edges of the handle hole to a good, smooth finish. Concentrate your efforts on the top of the hole, so the handle is easy and comfortable to hold.

8 Attach the router to its table, fit the ⅜ in. (10 mm) groove cutter and set the fence to 1 in. (25 mm). Run the two end boards and the side boards through to cut a groove ⅜ in. (10 mm) wide and ¼ in. (6 mm) deep, 1 in. (25 mm) up from the bottom edge (see Fig 8). Use a push-stick to feed the wood through and keep your fingers out of harm's way.

FIG 7

FIG 9

9 Do a dry run assembly in order to decide (by eye) how much the edges of the two end boards need to be angled back. Then pair the two boards back to back in the vice, and use the block plane to angle back from the mating faces (see Fig 9).

TIP

While in many ways this is an easy project to make, the final fitting of the base and sides is a bit of a challenge. In the first instance, it may help to put the whole holder together with short brads, perhaps with a friend's help, and then to adjust the various edges for the best fit. Angle the nails slightly so that they can't be pulled out easily.

FIG 10

10 Trim the plywood baseboard to fit your holder. Give all the component parts a quick sanding, then start nailing the whole thing together (see Fig 10). As the nailing progresses, you will see that the side and end boards cant (lean) out to the extent that the ¼ in. (6 mm) thick plywood base becomes a tight fit in the ⅜ in. (10 mm) wide grooves. You might even

need to ease the base by chamfering the edges of the routed grooves slightly. When the whole box is nailed together, give it a coat of paint on all surfaces.

When the paint is completely dry, sand selected faces and edges to cut through the paint. Concentrate your efforts on areas that would, in the normal course of events, receive the most wear.

Construction variations

Simple cut out handle

Battens nailed to base to make feet

Cut and shaped handle screwed to the side edges

Handle strip screwed to the side

V-shaped cut-away

Base shaped to fit inside sloping sides

RESOURCES

General suppliers

A & M Wood Specialty, Inc.
358 Eagle Street North
P.O. Box 3204
Cambridge, Ontario N3H 456
(519) 653-9322

Constantine's
2050 Eastchester Road
Bronx, NY 10461-2297
(800) 223-8087

Garret Wade
161 Avenue of the Americas
New York, NY 10213-0459
(800) 221-2942

Lee Valley & Veritas
1090 Morrison Drive
Ottawa, Ontario K2H 1C2

Leichtung Workshops
1108 N. Glen Road
Casper, WY 82601
(800) 321-6840

McFeeley's
P.O. Box 11169
Dept. AW6J
Lynchburg, VA 24506
(800) 443-7937

Rockler Woodworking and Hardware
4365 Willow Drive
Medina, MN 55340-9701
(800) 279-4441
www.rockler.com
Features woodworking and hardware products, on-line shopping, plans, store locators.

William Alden Company
27 Stuart Street
Boston, MA 02116
(800) 249-8665

Woodcraft
560 Airport Industrial Park
P.O. Box 1686
Parkersburg, WV 26102-1686

Woodworker's Supply of New Mexico
5604 Alameda Place
Albuquerque, NM 87113
(800) 645-9292

Finishing and upholstery supplier

Mohawk Finishing Products, Inc.
Rt. 30 North
Amsterdam, NY 12010
(800) 545-0047

Tool suppliers

Black & Decker Worldwide Headquarters
www.bdk.com
Site contains information on power tools.

International Tool Corp.
www.internationaltool.com
Features power tools for woodworkers, tips from experts, related links.

Klein Tools
www.kleintools.com
Contains product index and distributor locater.

McCally Tool & Supply
www.mccallytool.com
Site contains tool categories, accessories, on-line shopping.

Mytoolstore.com
www.mytoolstore.com
Contains hand and power tools, on-line shopping, expert advice.

The Stanley Works
www.stanleyworks.com
Site contains information about tools and where to purchase them.

The Tool Barn
www.thetoolbarn.com
Features hand tools for woodworkers, on-line shopping.

Hardware suppliers

The Hardware and Home Center Industry Resource Center
http://www.nrha.org/LINKS.html
Provides source for consumers to find hardware and related sites.

Restoration Hardware
www.restorationhardware.com
Contains hardware, customer service, and store locator.

Home Improvement Centers

Builder's Central
www.builderscentral.com
Features supplies, do-it-yourself manuals, on-line shopping.

Inside Spaces
www.insidespaces.com
Features how-to projects and tool dictionary.

Home & Workshop Online
www.johathanpress.com
Contains advertisers, links, and woodworking plans.

Lowe's Home Improvement Warehouse
www.lowes.com
Contains how-to library, on-line shopping, customer service, and store locator.

Wood suppliers

CyberYard Online Resources
www.cyberyard.com
Features wood library, terms glossary, ask the pros, resources.

Eco Timber
www.ecotimber.com
Distributor of ecological forest products. Site contains products, services, and sources.

EZ Wood
www.ezewood.com
Contains projects, on-line shopping catalogs, and links. Suppliers for hobbyists, carvers, and small woodworking shops.

Magazines

Fine Woodworking
63 S. Main Street
P.O. Box 5506
Newton, CT 06470-5506
(203) 426-8171
www.taunton.com/fw/index.html

Wood
1716 Locust Street
Des Moines, IA 50309-3023
www.woodmagazine.com

Woodwork
42 Digital Drive
Novato, CA 94949
(415) 382-0580

Workbench
www.workbenchmagazine.com

CONVERSION CHART

The metric measurements given in this book have been converted to imperial measurements by multiplying the metric figure given in the text by the relevant number shown in the table to the right. Bear in mind that conversions do not necessarily work out exactly, and some figures have been slightly rounded up or down. (Do not use a combination of metric and imperial measurements—for accuracy, keep to one system.)

To convert	*Multiply by*
millimeters to inches	0.0394
meters to feet	3.28
meters to yards	1.093
sq millimeters to sq inches	0.00155
sq meters to sq feet	10.76
sq meters to sq yards	1.195
cu meters to cu feet	35.31
cu meters to cu yards	1.308
grams to pounds	0.0022
kilograms to pounds	2.2046
liters to gallons	0.22

INDEX

page numbers for photographs and illustrations are shown in italics